THE RESURRECTION MEN

THE RESURRECTION MEN

A History of the Trade in Corpses

BRIAN BAILEY

Macdonald

A *Macdonald* Book

First published in Great Britain in 1991 by
Macdonald & Co (Publishers) Ltd
London & Sydney

British Library Cataloguing-in-Publication Data
Bailey, Brian
The resurrection men.
I. Title
364.1

ISBN 0-356-21050-3

Photoset in North Wales by
Derek Doyle & Associates, Mold, Clwyd
Printed and bound in Great Britain by
BPCC Hazell Books
Aylesbury, Bucks, England
Member of BPCC Ltd.

Macdonald & Co (Publishers) Ltd
165 Great Dover Street
London SE1 4YA
A member of Maxwell Macmillan Publishing Corporation

'About this time there arose a great sough and
surmise, that some loons were playing false with
the kirkyard, howking up the bodies from their damp
graves, and harling them away to the College. Words
cannot describe the fear, and the dool, and the misery
it caused. All flocked to the kirk-yett; and the
friends of the newly buried stood by the mools, which
were yet dark, and the brown newly cast divots, that
had not yet taken root, looking, with mournful faces,
to descry any tokens of sinking in.'

David Macbeth Moir
The Life of Mansie Wauch, 1824

Contents

Introduction

The seventy-five-year period between the eighteenth- and nineteenth-century appearances of Halley's comet was a time when Britain was on the threshold of new standards of triumph and civilization. Captain Cook made important discoveries on the far side of the earth. Napoleon was defeated by Nelson at sea and by Wellington on land. The rise of manufacturing industry and the beginning of the railway revolution were accompanied by the abolition of slavery and the reforms of prison and factory conditions by men such as William Wilberforce, John Howard and Robert Owen. The Adam brothers brought new architectural elegance to London and Edinburgh. It was the age of Gainsborough and Turner, Edward Gibbon and Sir Walter Scott, Jane Austen and Sarah Siddons, Wordsworth and Sheridan, Burns and Shelley.

Beneath Georgian Britain's classical gloss, however, was a very different order – a world of poverty and urban slums, whence, in the midnight hours, men crept out to dig up bodies from churchyards, and offered them for sale for a few shillings to educated gentlemen, who would not only purchase the stark and pallid corpses, but gave every encouragement to the sellers to increase their labours.

The fashionable and elegant façade of Georgian society preferred not to know too much about the horrors going on in this underworld. There were those who protested that accounts of such incidents ought not to be published in the newspapers, and often the press did refrain from printing all the facts. The rich did not want to read the ghastly details of lower class breaches of common decency, which were only to be expected from such people, and which did not concern *them*. And even those whose duty it was to govern the country showed little inclination to soil their minds with such sordid matters, staying away from the House of Commons when the subject was debated.

This is the full story of that repellent period of our history. Only a hundred and fifty years later, it seems scarcely believable that such things could have gone on in a modern 'civilized' country. I have tried to tell the tale dispassionately, without the hysteria that characterized much public reaction at the time, or the sensationalism that has accompanied accounts of it since (often concentrating on the murders that were inevitable consequences of the trade, rather than on the trade itself). The truth is unquestionably gruesome, but the story is a part of our relatively recent social history that needs to be told seriously, if only to remind us that the evils which can grow from social and political circumstances are not the exclusive prerogatives of wicked foreigners. Body-snatching was a peculiarly British practice.

Some of the exploits of resurrection men I have chosen to include are based on hearsay and frequent repetition. Where there are contemporary reports and reliable later accounts, I have given my sources in the Notes to the chapters at the end of the book.

Acknowledgments

My grateful thanks are due to Mr I.F. Lyle and his staff at the Library of the Royal College of Surgeons of England, for enabling me to consult valuable material in the College's possession, and for their help with the illustrations.

Professor M.H. Kaufman of Edinburgh University Medical School also gave me particular help with the illustrations, and I am grateful for his kind co-operation.

I am deeply indebted to the local history departments of a number of libraries for their help with my researches, and I list them in alphabetical order: Bristol, Exeter, Glasgow, Leeds, Liverpool, Manchester, Newcastle-on-Tyne, Norwich, Portsmouth and Sheffield.

My thanks are also due to the Public Record Office and the House of Lords Library; to H.M. Inspector of Anatomy for helpful information; to Ralph Brooke and Paul Gunnion; and especially to my wife for her help with the photographs and the typescript, and for her general support and endless patience.

List of Illustrations

1 *The Anatomy Lesson of Dr Johannes Deijman* by Rembrandt, 1656. Much of this painting was destroyed by fire in 1723, but the central part remains, showing the dissected corpse of Joris Fonteyn, who had been hanged for theft.

Rijksmuseum, Amsterdam

2 *The Reward of Cruelty* by Hogarth, 1750. In Britain the bodies of executed murderers were frequently handed over to surgeons for dissection. Hogarth's etching was intended to expose the barbarity of the times, but soon after it was done, the law decreed that *all* murderers' bodies should be 'anatomized'.

Mansell Collection

3 Amputation of a leg at the thigh. This graphic drawing leaves no room for doubt about the importance of a thorough knowledge of anatomy for surgeons. Before the discovery of anaesthesia, speed was of the essence.

By kind permission of the Royal College of Surgeons

4 Haworth churchyard, West Yorkshire. It was 'so filled with graves,' Charlotte Brontë wrote, 'that the rank weeds and coarse grass scarce had room to shoot up between the monuments.' It was typical of the state

of overcrowded graveyards in the early nineteenth century.

Photograph: Rita Bailey

5   *The Resurrectionists* by Rowlandson. This contemporary water colour captures some of the ghastly spirit of the business well enough, but only the early amateurs would have dug up the entire coffin.

By kind permission of the Royal College of Surgeons

6   The 'resurrection corkscrew' at Salcombe Regis, Devon. The tool now used as the bolt on the churchyard gate was left behind by two fleeing body-snatchers. It was originally longer, with a 'corkscrew' end which was driven into coffin lids.

Photograph: Rita Bailey

7   The 'resurrection stone' at Pannal, North Yorkshire. One of the earliest precautions against body-snatchers was to lower a huge stone like this over the coffin. Too heavy to be lifted by two or three men, it could be removed by block-and-tackle when the grave was safe from disturbance, and used again.

Photograph: Ralph Brooke

8   Iron mort-safes in Greyfriars churchyard, Edinburgh. Enclosing graves in heavy iron cages like these was an alternative form of defence. They were often moved from one grave to another, being hired out by the week.

By courtesy of Edinburgh City Libraries

9   The 'body-snatchers' cage' at Henham, Essex. Iron mort-safes were less common in England than in Scotland (where they were invented), but this one remains in a village churchyard susceptible, no doubt, to visits by London resurrection men.

Photograph: Rita Bailey

10   Frenchay, Avon. The heavy stone slab on top of this grave in the churchyard is bolted down, in what was obviously a private arrangement, not intended to be hired out to anyone else, even when the corpse was safe.
Photograph: Rita Bailey

11   Sir Astley Paston Cooper, Bart. Elected President of the Royal College of Surgeons in 1827, and Vice-President of the Royal Society in 1830, one of his less flattering titles was 'King of the Resurrectionists'.
By kind permission of the Royal College of Surgeons

12   Parish reward, Bristol. This poster offering a reward for information leading to the conviction of body-snatchers appeared in Bristol in 1819 after a woman's body was taken from St Augustine's churchyard.
Bristol Record Office (in the collection of Bristol Royal Infirmary)

13   Dissection at Liverpool. This drawing by Alexander Mosses shows a corpse being dissected by John and James Cooper in the early 1820s. John Cooper was a surgeon, but James was apparently a music teacher!
Liverpool City Libraries

14 Watch tower in New Calton Burial Ground, Edinburgh. The three-storey castellated tower was one of the most elaborate of the buildings erected during the body-snatching period to facilitate constant guarding of fresh graves.
Royal Commission on Ancient Monuments, Scotland

15   Warblington, Hampshire. A small watch-hut of flint and brick, one of two erected at opposite corners of the parish churchyard.
Photograph: Rita Bailey

16   Bill for Dr Knox's course of lectures for the autumn and winter season of 1828–9 at 10 Surgeons' Square, Edinburgh. Note that an 'ample supply of Anatomical Subjects' was promised.
Department of Anatomy, Edinburgh University

17   The remains of William Burke. The skeleton of the notorious murderer was preserved after his execution and dissection in 1829. Note the sawn-off skull.
Department of Anatomy, Edinburgh University

18   Dr Robert Knox. A rare photograph of Knox, showing him lecturing in his fiftieth year, long after the Burke and Hare scandal.
Courtesy of the Royal College of Surgeons of Edinburgh

19   Elizabeth Ross or Cook. This drawing by W.H. Clift was made when the corpse was delivered to the Royal College of Surgeons after her execution for murder in 1832. The woman was reputed to be a body-snatcher.
By kind permission of the Royal College of Surgeons

Chapter I: A Necessary Evil

'I will stamp him into a cullis, flay off his skin, to cover one of the anatomies this rogue hath set i' the cold yonder in Barber-Chirurgeon's Hall.'

John Webster
The Duchess of Malfi, 1623

On 5 December 1831, before an hysterical mob estimated by one observer to number thirty thousand, two men were brought out to the scaffold in front of London's Newgate Gaol and hanged by the executioner, William Calcraft. Their bodies were then handed over, as was the custom, for dissection by surgeons, in a classic case of 'the biter bit'.

John Bishop and Thomas Williams had been convicted of murdering an Italian boy, Carlo Ferrari. Their motive was to earn a few guineas by selling the corpse to the anatomy school at King's College. They duly delivered the body, on a Saturday afternoon in the centre of the nation's capital city, in a straw hamper which they had hired a street porter to carry for them.

Bishop and Williams brought close to home an evil which had been growing like a cancer in society for more than half a century without any firm decision being taken to excise it. Ten days after their execution, a Bill was introduced in the House of Commons to

1

regulate schools of anatomy. It became law within a few months. It was not intended as legislation against murder, which had always, of course, been a capital crime. Its intention was to put an end to a crime for which murder had become a logical extension – the robbery of graves, or *body-snatching*.

Not that grave-robbery was a new invention of the late-Georgian criminal community. Indeed, it has some claim to be regarded as one of the oldest offences against humanity. The ancient Egyptians presented irresistible opportunities to thieves by burying their illustrious dead with rich treasures, protected only by the challenge to the criminal mind of finding them in labyrinthine burial chambers. And bodies, as well as gold and jewels, were stolen in the ancient world, for the extremities of the dead were used in black magic. Robert Graves and Joshua Podro suggested that the body of Jesus was guarded after its burial, not to prevent his disciples from taking him away, as Matthew stated, but to prevent grave-robbers from despoiling the body of its extremities.[1] Lucan wrote in the first century AD: 'When the dead are confined in stone, then the witch eagerly vents her savagery on all the limbs, scooping out the stiffened eye-balls, gnawing the yellow nails on the withered hands ...'[2]

Crucified criminals in the Roman world were liable, whilst still hanging on their crosses, to be mutilated by practitioners of the occult arts. Apuleius describes one of the rituals of the enchantress Pamphilae: 'She had everything ready there for her deadly rites; all sorts of aromatic incense, metal plaques engraved with secret signs, beaks and claws of ill-omened birds, various bits of corpse-flesh – in one place she had arranged the noses and fingers of crucified men, in another the nails that had been driven through their palms and ankles, with bits of flesh still sticking to them – also little bladders of life-blood saved from the men she had murdered and the skulls of criminals who had been thrown to the wild beasts in the amphitheatre.'[3]

From Tacitus to Shakespeare we get similar recipes for the practice of black magic. The Roman general Germanicus, father of Caligula, died at Antioch with the remains of human bodies on the floor of his bedroom, along with spells, curses and other 'malignant objects which are supposed to consign souls to the powers of the tomb.'[4] And the Scotch broth of the witches in *Macbeth* testifies to the survival of belief in such practices after more than fifteen hundred years – 'Liver of blaspheming Jew … Nose of Turk, and Tartar's lips; finger of birth-strangled babe …' and other such delectable ingredients. Necromancy played some part in the witch-craze of the sixteenth and seventeenth centuries, and werewolves, according to the Jacobean dramatist John Webster, 'Steal forth to churchyards in the dead of night, and dig dead bodies up.'[5]

At the famous trial of the so-called Witches of Pendle in Lancashire in 1612, when twenty convicted witches were hanged, witnesses swore on oath that some of the women accused of bewitching local people 'by devilish practices and hellish means' had dug up corpses from local graveyards and taken their teeth and scalps. The evidence may have been the false testimony of mass hysteria, but it attests to the currency of the idea at the time.

So the robbing of graves – a by-product of the social custom of disposing of the dead by inhumation – was a crime with a very long pedigree. It had always been regarded with horror as one of the most heinous of crimes, indeed in the time of Constantine the Great, one of the few grounds on which a woman could obtain a divorce was if her husband was a grave-robber. The Church, however, gave some fresh impetus to exhumation when the Holy Inquisition took to the digging up of heretics it wished to disgrace by mutilating their corpses. The remains of John Wycliffe were raised from consecrated ground at Lutterworth more than forty years after his death, and burnt in a symbolic act of punishment for his opinions. And the secular authority, taking the ecclesiastical hint, took the body of Oliver Cromwell from its burial place in Westminster Abbey, two years after his death, and hanged it on the gallows at Tyburn, before severing the head to expose it at Westminster Hall and flinging the body into a pit. Richard III's remains were likewise exhumed at the dissolution of the monasteries and thrown into the River Soar at Leicester.

Bodies were occasionally mutilated for quite different reasons. When Frederick Barbarossa, the German emperor, was drowned in 1190 during a crusade, his corpse was cut up and boiled to separate the flesh from the bones, so that the latter could be returned for Christian burial in his native land rather than be committed to Muslim soil.

Thus there was no lack of precedent for anything the modern body-snatchers were to do. But the revival of exhumation as a profitable business in an ostensibly civilized state was a glaring condemnation of the social condition of Georgian Britain. The underworld was presented with motive, opportunity and method for an outrage which ought to have been an almost forgotten memory of barbarism. The motive was financial gain; the opportunity was presented by the state of medical knowledge and research; the method was made easy by the appalling condition of urban churchyards.

In order to place the modern resurgence of grave-robbery in its proper context, and understand its causes, it is necessary to consider the medical background of the period, and in particular the study of anatomy. In the Europe of Elizabeth I's time, medical practice and witchcraft were not far apart. Among physicians, there was a growing body of opinion that powerful and effective medicines could be prepared from the human body, and text-books of the time recommended such remedies as powdered human bone in red wine for rheumatism, and prepared human skull for epilepsy. 'Moss from the skull of a man hung in chains,' one manual asserted, 'is a haemostatic.'

What difference was there between these doctors' remedies and the old wives' beliefs that a newborn baby's life expectancy could be told from an examination of the afterbirth; or that a variety of maladies could be cured merely by a touch from the reigning monarch? Was it magic or psychology that cured a man who believed himself possessed by an evil spirit? He recovered when a doctor surreptitiously let a live bat out of a bag at the same moment as a surgeon made a tiny incision in the patient's side and a priest ordered the devil to fly out.[6]

The growth of scientific method could only gradually supersede such age-old superstitions. William Harvey published his *Anatomical Disquisition on the Motion of the Heart and Blood* in 1628, but the full significance of his discovery was not grasped for a long time. 'It seemed to illustrate the theory of medicine,' as one commentator wrote, 'yet it made no improvement in the practice thereof.'[7] The antiquary John Aubrey, who was a pall-bearer at Harvey's funeral, wrote: 'I have heard him say, that after his Booke of the Circulation of the Blood came-out, that he fell mightily in his Practize, and that 'twas beleeved by the vulgar that he was crack-brained; and all the physitians were against his Opinion, and envyed him: many wrote against him. With much adoe at last, in about 20 or 30 yeares time, it was recived in all the Universities of the world ...'[8]

Nevertheless, important advances in the knowledge of anatomy and physiology were constantly being made in the seventeenth century, and scientific medicine began to replace the cures of wise women, quacks and magicians. Robert Hooke's work with the microscope contributed to the new interest in investigation of the healthy body and the changes wrought by disease, and treatment by scientific methods led to the foundation of an increasing number of voluntary hospitals in the following century.

As for anatomy in particular, the ancient Egyptians had studied it under the Ptolemies, and even credited one of their early kings with having written a treatise on the subject some four thousand years before the birth of Christ. Herophilus and Erasistratus were anatomists of repute in the city of Alexandria, but we have no record of the extent of their knowledge. It is clear from the known methods of mummification that the Egyptians had an extensive knowledge of the contents of the bodily cavities, but we do not know how far they understood the functions of the various organs. It is probable, however, that ancient Egypt had considerably more such first-hand knowledge than medieval Europe.

In the Middle Ages, anatomy was taught only as a theoretical subject. The word of the Greek anatomist Galen, who had been state physician to the Emperor Marcus Aurelius, was law for thirteen centuries. The absence of practical demonstration before the late fifteenth century was due to superstitions and religious taboos against opening up the human body, where spirits were believed to reside. Pope Boniface VIII forbade the dissection of human bodies in 1300 AD on the grounds that they were the images of God. Throughout Europe, the Church placed an interdict on the dissection of corpses, since the resurrection of the body, as opposed to the immortality of the soul, was one of its central dogmas. So the only experience of human anatomy had been gained from the ancient practice of embalming and an occasional post mortem examination when there was some doubt about the cause of death of important people. A manual of autopsy, consisting of a mere forty pages, was published in Bologna in 1316.

The modern study of anatomy was placed on a scientific foundation by the great Belgian anatomist Vesalius (Andre van Wezel), who published his famous *De humani corporis fabrica* in 1543, based on the dissection of human corpses rather than those of animals, from which earlier anatomists, including Galen, had been forced to draw their inferences. The dissection of barbary apes and other animals had put surgeons on a par with the average butcher in terms of their knowledge of human anatomy. Vesalius obtained his own first skeleton by stealing the body of a hanged man from outside the city walls of Louvain.

Leonardo da Vinci, according to his own testimony, dissected more than thirty human corpses in the late fifteenth and early sixteenth centuries. He studied anatomy from the artist's point of view, and then went considerably further to make drawings of the structure of the heart and skull, and one of the earliest representations of an embryo in the womb. Around 1500 AD, Leonardo carried out an autopsy on a hundred-year-old man at the hospital of Sta Maria Nuova in Florence, and Vasari tells us that he collaborated in his studies with Marc Antonio della Torre, who lectured on anatomy at Pavia.[9] But Pope Leo X put an end to Leonardo's research.[10]

Michelangelo and other Italian artists also dissected human corpses, and one of the beneficial consequences of the Renaissance artists' interest in anatomy was that the medical treatise of Vesalius was beautifully and accurately illustrated, probably by John de Calcar, a pupil of Titian.

Another artist who studied anatomy for himself was the English painter George Stubbs. He was born in Liverpool in 1724, and it is sometimes said that his father was a surgeon, though he is more usually described as a currier. George certainly retained a life-long interest in anatomy, and before turning his attention to the horse, for which he became justly famous, he dissected human subjects, and was for a time a lecturer on anatomy to medical students in York. Details of his early life are scant, but in the circumstances of the time, it has to be seen as a probability that Stubbs either had connections with body-snatchers, or indeed was one himself.

During the course of the seventeenth century, the work of Dutch biologists gradually brought Leiden University to the forefront of medical research, displacing Padua, where both Vesalius and Harvey had studied, as the leading centre in Europe. Great advances were made by men such as Boerhaave and de Graaf, whilst Pieter Paauw was the great Dutch leader in the study of anatomy. The pre-eminence of Leiden was due to several factors, not least of which was the hunger for learning in the proud new Dutch republic, and, more specifically, the skill of the Dutch in making microscopes.

Before the sixteenth century, Padua and Leiden were the only two universities where anatomy could be studied, with the result that medical students came to Leiden from all over the world, including Britain. The Protestant United Provinces, even under the influence of Calvinism, were more tolerant of scientific research and experiment than the Catholic countries. Thus Leiden had a particular attraction for students from Scotland, Calvinism being one of the forces that formed strong links between the Scots and the Dutch.

The practices prevailing in the early teaching of anatomy in the United Provinces were generally those, therefore, that crossed the North Sea to become established in Britain. Amsterdam had seen the legal dissection of human subjects since 1555, when what we now call Holland was still part of the Spanish Netherlands. King Philip had granted the Guild of Surgeons there the privilege of receiving once a year for dissection the corpse of a criminal sentenced to death by the city's judges and lawfully executed. The annual anatomy demonstration became a popular public event, and invariably began with a dissection of the abdominal cavity. The lecturers were titled 'Praelector' or *reader* in anatomy, because before being allowed to dissect corpses, they simply read out the texts of Galen.

Paauw founded the anatomy theatre at Leiden in 1592, modelling it on the classical amphitheatre – ironically enough, for anatomy lectures were attended by an eager public with something akin to the appreciation of spectators in the Roman circus watching living people being torn apart by wild animals. Paauw is said to have dissected about sixty corpses – all of them male – in the course of his twenty-two years as professor of anatomy at Leiden. (The first Dutch dissection of a female corpse was reputedly done by Frederick Ruysch in Amsterdam in 1720.) There are many representations by Dutch artists of these occasions, of which Rembrandt's are by far the most famous and accomplished. Opposition to such dissection was more often fuelled by emotion than by logic. Hugo de Groot, the famous jurist, wrote: 'Antiquity knew not these torture-chambers of the dead, where these unnecessary cruelties are practised by the living upon the dead.'

That a similar situation prevailed in Edinburgh by the seventeenth century is shown by an incident in 1678, when the body of a gypsy executed for murder disappeared from its grave in Greyfriars churchyard. Some thought the man had come back to life, but others were sure he had been stolen by a surgeon, 'to make an anatomical dissection of', as one contemporary put it, 'which was criminal to take at their own hande, since the magistrates would not have refused it, and I hear the chirurgeons afferme, the town of Edinburgh is obliged to give them a malefactor's body once a year for that effect.' It was also usual in Paris and Leiden by then, the writer added, for criminals' bodies to be given to the surgeons, 'also some of them that dyes in hospitals'. In fact, the surgeons of Edinburgh had been granted the body of 'ane condampnit man' a year since 1505, when the town council had first granted a charter to the Incorporation of Surgeons and Barbers.

The first published work on anatomy in English – still based on Galen and Aristotle – was the 1548 *Anatomie of the Bodie of Man* by Thomas Vicary. But it was over a hundred years before the country's first anatomical theatre was opened by the College of Physicians, in Knight Rider Street near St Paul's Cathedral. Surgeons were slowly earning a degree of public regard, though not equal to that in which physicians were held. The latter were considered superior, as men of learning, while surgeons were mere manual workers, who found it hard to shake off their old association with barbers, for whom blood-letting had been the universal remedy for all complaints. The Company of Barber-Surgeons had been founded in the reign of Henry VIII, and surgeons did not officially part company with barbers until 1745. Surgeons were getting many corpses for dissection unofficially at that time, ten shillings and sixpence being paid to the Constable of Holborn for every body delivered to them from the gallows at Tyburn.

John Stow recorded a 'strange thing' in London at the end of the sixteenth century, when a man 'hanged for felonie at Saint Thomas Waterines, being begged by the Chirurgeons of London, to have made of him an anatomie after he was dead to all men's thinking, cut downe, throwne into a carre, and so brought from the place of execution through the Borough of Southwarke over the bridge, and through the citie of London to the Chirurgeons Hall nere unto Cripelgate: The chest being opened there, and the weather extreme cold hee was found to be alive, and lived till the three and twentie of Februarie, and then died.'[11]

Surgery had as little basis in science as did execution. John Hunter, the eighteenth-century Scottish anatomist and one of the founders of modern scientific surgery, could still describe the average surgeon as 'a savage armed with a knife', and surgery was only undertaken as a last resort. But increasing urban populations in the early years of the industrial revolution, with their attendant diseases and accidents, created a demand for larger numbers of qualified physicians and surgeons. Proper medical attention was no longer the prerogative of the wealthy, partly because the rich depended on having fit workers to create their wealth, and the study of anatomy was now recognized as a vital part of the training of skilled medical men.

Before the discovery of anaesthesia in the nineteenth century, the skill and dexterity of surgeons was paramount in performing operations in which speed was the most essential factor. Strong men had to hold down struggling and shrieking patients who were as liable to die from shock under the knife as from the diseases that necessitated their operations. Only the surgeon's speed could afford the unfortunate patient any relief from the agony and terror of being operated on whilst fully conscious, held or strapped down on a

bloody wooden table. The senses might be dulled by
opium or alcohol, but from the moment of the first
incision, every fraction of a second was an unspeakable
torture. The Scottish surgeon Robert Liston became
famous for the high speed of his operations. He could
amputate a leg at the thigh in less than thirty seconds,
including completion of the ligatures. Such speed
depended on complete confidence in what one was
doing, and only a thorough knowledge of the anatomy
of the human body could provide that.

The study of anatomy was hampered by one great
drawback, however, and that was the lack of sufficient
subjects for dissection. The law in Christian Europe had
for centuries allowed only the bodies of executed
criminals to be used for lectures on anatomy.[12] One of
the students at Leiden in the early eighteenth century
was Alexander Monro, who played a major role in
establishing Edinburgh as the leading medical school in
Britain. Three Alexander Monros, father, son and
grandson, held the chair of anatomy at Edinburgh for
126 continuous years (though not with equal distinction).

The school had been founded by Alexander
Monteith, who at the end of the seventeenth century,
had been granted permission to receive bodies for dissection, after petitioning the town council to allow him to
open the bodies of 'poor persons who die in Paul's
Workhouse, and have none to bury them'. Monteith
dangled in front of the council the ambitious promise
that, if so permitted, he would make 'better improve-
ments in anatomy in a short time than have been made
by Leyden in thirty years'. The Edinburgh Faculty put
forward a rival application, proposing the grant of 'the
bodies of foundlings who dye betwixt the time that they
are weaned and their being put to schools and trades;
also the bodies of such as are dead-born, which are

exposed; also, suicides, a violent death, and have none to own them; likewise the bodies of such as are put to death by sentence of the magistrates.'

Both these applications were granted, on condition that the intestines of all bodies received were buried within two days, and the rest within ten days. But the demand for subjects was, throughout the country, far greater than the supply. It was a classic dilemma which the law of the land failed to resolve, largely because of pressure from the Church. As the Napoleonic wars began, towards the end of the eighteenth century, the need for skilled surgeons for the army and navy grew ever more urgent, yet the medical schools were denied the means of teaching them properly. The government's double standards meant that, as Sir Astley Cooper, President of the Royal College of Surgeons, was to put it later, an ignorant surgeon 'must mangle the living if he has not operated on the dead'.

The extent of the problem was peculiar to Britain, for other countries were groping their way towards satisfactory answers to the need for trained surgeons, and the medical schools of civilized nations were not handicapped by unresponsive governments. Thus while body-snatching was a widespread and profitable activity in Britain, the practice never extended elsewhere, since there was no incentive for it, although it was not unknown in America, where the laws varied from state to state and in some of them body-snatching was a vital source of supply.

The anatomists of Germany, for instance, were permitted to receive the bodies of suicides and prostitutes, as well as executed criminals. The doctors of France were well supplied with subjects in the late eighteenth-century and after by Madame Guillotine, and subsequently by the receipt of corpses unclaimed by friends or relatives: the dead washed up by the Seine in

Paris, or those found dead in the streets – corpses such as those laid out for identification in the Paris Morgue, described so vividly by Zola.[13] Bodies were so easily available in Paris, in fact, that the dissecting rooms of La Pitié Hôpital had around a dozen a day, and those who wanted to sell corpses to the medical schools could get no more than five francs.

'Behind La Pitié,' wrote the English surgeon John Green Crosse in 1815, 'are three dissecting rooms which contain 90 tables and in each room an articulated skeleton is set up. The first of the three great rooms I entered contained 23 cadavres and nearly four times as many students. All the bodies that die at l'Hôtel Dieu are regularly brought to these rooms to be dissected and, when they have been converted to this rational purpose, the débris are as regularly taken away for burial.'

In Holland, Austria and Italy, also, body-snatching was unknown, because the governments of these countries made proper provision for the teaching of anatomy by allowing bodies unclaimed by relatives or friends to be used for that purpose. In Portugal, where there was a high rate of infant mortality, surgeons could obtain an ample supply of corpses quite legally, and resurrection men were unheard of.

In Britain, however, medical men continued to be trained, if not within the law, then outside it, and those in authority turned a blind eye on the matter for most of the time. Body-snatching was but one evil among many, and by no means – at first – the most urgently in need of suppression; or so it seemed to those who governed. Late Georgian Britain was a country in some danger of becoming ungovernable. The government was made up largely of land-owning country squires, and law and order was in the hands of parish constables hopelessly unequal to the task. Both systems had been rendered out of date by the industrial revolution, which resulted in a huge increase in urban population without the far-reaching social reforms needed to cope with it. The population of England almost doubled during the course of the eighteenth century, and by far the greatest growth was in the manufacturing towns such as Manchester, Birmingham, Bristol and Leeds.

Well-meaning men founded a Society for Reformation of the Manners of the Lower Orders, whilst the coarseness and licentiousness of the aristocracy was the worst of any age in Britain. There was a rapid growth of town and city slums with their attendant diseases and high rates of infant mortality, and crime mushroomed with the overcrowding and poverty. Gin shops proliferated. The government's answer to these problems was to extend the death penalty even to petty crimes, and life became cheap. Society's consequent callousness and brutality was a breeding ground for many evils, and the machinery of government was too slow and incompetent to deal with them properly.

The condition of British churchyards at that time was such that obtaining a fresh corpse was a relatively easy matter, and it is a nice irony that the Church, which led the strong opposition to legal dissection, also provided the means of its illegal practice. For hundreds of years the dead of each parish had been buried on top of one another in churchyards so that the ground level of the graves had gradually risen well above the foundations of the churches, a fact which can readily be confirmed by looking at almost any old churchyard today. In urban areas, the rapid increase in population during the eighteenth century, combined with a high death rate resulting from slum conditions, inadequate sanitation and gin drinking, led to churchyards becoming so overcrowded that they were a major cause of concern to health authorities.

As long ago as 1726 a Church of England clergyman, Revd T. Lewis, published pamphlets on the 'Indecent and Dangerous Custom' of burial in churches and churchyards, and its 'Profaneness, Indecency, and Pernicious Consequences to the Living'. By 1804, France had forbidden all further burials in its city churchyards, but in Britain nothing was done, and the situation became increasingly horrific. One London churchyard of less than an acre in size received fourteen thousand bodies in the course of twenty years. No wonder grave-diggers had to get drunk before they could face their jobs, and sometimes buried corpses only two or three feet deep because of obstruction by old coffins and the quantity of bones in the soil. Mention by John Aubrey of the fact that Samuel Butler, the satirist and author of *Hudibras*, was buried in the churchyard at Covent Garden in 1680 'by his desire 6 foot deepe'[14] shows that such depth was exceptional at that time.

In Yorkshire, Charlotte Brontë remarked of her father's churchyard at Haworth that it was 'so filled with graves that the rank weeds and coarse grass scarce had room to shoot up between the monuments' and Charles Dickens skilfully sketched the condition of a London churchyard in *Bleak House*:

> There! says Jo, pointing, Over yinder, among them pile of bones, and close to that there kitchin winder! They put him very nigh the top. They was obliged to stamp upon it to git it in. I could unkiver it for you with my broom, if the gate was open. That's why they locks it, I s'pose, giving it a shake. It's always locked. Look at the rat! cries Jo, excited. Hi! Look! There he goes! Ho! Into the ground.

George Walker, a London surgeon, founded a Society for the Abolition of Burial in Towns, and published a book in which he detailed the 'dangerous and fatal results produced by the Unwise and revolting custom of inhuming the Dead in the midst of the Living.' Sir Edwin Chadwick also concluded from his influential investigation into the country's sanitation that 'all interments in towns, where bodies decompose, contribute to the mass of atmospheric impurity which is injurious to the public health.'

Walker described how, in the case of one particular grave, 'A body, partly decomposed, was dug up, and placed on the surface, at the side, slightly covered with earth; a mourner stepped upon it, the loosened skin peeled off, he slipped forward, and had nearly fallen into the grave.' The bones and bodies frequently dug up by grave-diggers were thrown into charnel houses, often the crypts of churches, where they could remain piled up and rotting for many years. Dickens remarked that 'rot and mildew and dead citizens' formed the uppermost scent in London's churches.[15] And it was a frequent practice of sextons and undertakers to store the corpses of still-born babies in their houses until a sufficient number had been accumulated to justify the digging of a grave for their mass burial.

When grave-diggers broke open coffins with their spades during digging, as they frequently did in overcrowded churchyards, they would instantly retire some distance for a while until the nauseous and noxious gases had dispersed a little in the air.

A London grave-digger named Miller, giving evidence in 1842 to a Select Committee enquiring into the problem of burial in towns, was asked, 'Were you in the habit of performing this grave-digging without the use of spirits?'

'No,' he replied, 'we were obliged to be half groggy to do it, and we cheered one another and sung to one another.'

'You found the work so disgusting that you were

obliged to be half drunk?'

'Yes.'

Open sewers and the absence of piped water permitted matter from decomposing bodies under the ground to seep into wells and streams, and the cholera epidemics of the nineteenth century were blamed by some on the urban churchyards. Walker referred to black flies emerging from coffins in vast numbers in warm weather, and infesting a chapel where children attending Sunday School christened them 'body bugs'.

Paupers' graves, called 'poor holes', were especially disgraceful, though profitable sources of supply for the resurrection men. These pits, as described by a correspondent of the *Public Advertiser* in April 1774, 'capable of holding three or four coffins abreast and about seven in depth; are always kept open till they are full, then the tops are covered over with earth; and another pit about the same size is dug on the side of it, leaving the sides of the former coffins always open.'

The appalling state of churchyards facilitated the desecration of graves for acts other than the stealing of newly buried corpses. Bones were stolen for grinding down to be sold as manure, and coffins were dug up for use as firewood. Sometimes grave-diggers themselves stole the metal fittings from coffins before filling in the graves, to supplement their meagre incomes. In 1732, a grave-digger named Loftus was charged with 'robbing of dead corpses' and confessed to the plunder of more than fifty graves. Those investigated were found with naked corpses in them, 'some mangled in so horrible a manner as could scarcely be supposed to be done by a human creature.' Loftus had stolen not only the coffins and burial clothes, but also the fat from the corpses, obtaining a good price for it, probably from chandlers.

The remains of the poet John Milton were savaged by souvenir hunters when his tomb at St Giles, Cripplegate, was opened in 1790 during building work on the church. Teeth were loosened from the jaw by knocking them with a stone, and a leg-bone was removed. Afterwards, a woman grave-digger, Elizabeth Grant, is said to have charged sixpence a time for showing the remains to curious visitors.[16]

Thus the stage was set for one of the most repulsive dramas in the history of what we are pleased to call civilization in Britain. The latter years of the eighteenth century saw the growth of profitable trading in dead bodies, in which outwardly respectable surgeons and professors were, perforce, the willing and indeed eager accessories after, and often before, the fact. Every society suffers the crime it deserves, however, and there can hardly be any doubt, with the benefit of hindsight, that the fiendish characters who came to be known as the 'resurrection men' were a necessary evil. These monsters of barbarism, whom the doctors habitually represented as the 'scum of the earth', were as essential as the doctors themselves in conferring the benefits of medical science on the population at large.

Chapter II: Exploratory Medicine

'Who shall conceive the horrors of my secret toil, as I dabbled among the unhallowed damps of the grave ...?'

Mary Shelley
Frankenstein, 1818

The professors of anatomy needed fresh corpses – the fresher the better. A corpse in an advanced state of decomposition is of no use for teaching purposes, and a corpse that had been buried for a month or more was in no danger of being dug up for medical purposes. The requirement for fresh bodies was eventually to present the criminal underworld with an opportunity to make money, and the need for medical knowledge was to lead the finest teachers and surgeons of the time into an uneasy alliance with the criminal community. But before the professional criminal caught on to this lucrative trade, surgeons and their students had to procure subjects for themselves. Medical students had a half-century's tradition of robbing graves to supply their teachers with subjects for dissection.

Not that the stealing of dead bodies was a serious crime at that time. Stealing a shroud or a coffin was a felony, but stealing a corpse was only a misdemeanour. Until 1788 it was not even that, since the law held that a dead body was nobody's property. In 1795, Sir John Frederick introduced a Bill to Parliament for making the

21

stealing of a corpse a felony, but it was thrown out. So the experienced body-snatcher always stripped a corpse naked before removing it from the churchyard, so as to be convicted only of the lesser offence if apprehended.

This extraordinary circumstance perhaps requires some explanation. The blossoming of the industrial revolution led to great social changes for which governments were ill prepared. The rapidly growing urban population was inevitably afflicted with appalling poverty and consequently there was a huge increase in crime. At the same time the tendency of the better-off was towards greater materialism and personal wealth. Crime was seen mainly as a threat to private property, and dealing with it was the chief pre-occupation of local authorities. Those who were powerful and wealthy believed that there was a 'criminal class' which must be virtually eliminated if society was to survive. Thus the so-called 'Bloody Code' was born, which by 1819 listed more than two hundred offences punishable by death. These included associating with gypsies, impersonating a pensioner of Greenwich Hospital, writing a threatening letter, and appearing on a highway with a sooty face; but the vast majority of capital offences related directly to the protection of property. A person – man, woman or child – could be hanged for stealing turnips, shooting a rabbit, picking a pocket, damaging a fish-pond, cutting down a tree or setting fire to a haystack.

Crimes against property were the obsession of Georgian criminal law. In 1772, a boy was hanged at Tyburn for attempted housebreaking. In 1800, a boy of ten was sentenced to death for secreting notes in a post office. In the following year, a thirteen-year-old boy was hanged for stealing a spoon, and in 1808 a girl of seven was hanged in Norfolk. The brutality and insensitivity of Georgian society was all-pervading. It was in 1810 that the Lord Chief Justice, Lord Ellenborough, made his notorious speech against the abolition of the death penalty for stealing up to the value of five shillings from a shop. If the Bill went through, he said, no man would be able to 'trust himself for an hour out of doors without the most alarming apprehensions, that, on his return, every vestige of his property will be swept off by the hardened robber.'

Crimes against the person took a back seat during this period of deplorable materialism. Even attempted murder was only a misdemeanour before 1803. So removing a dead body, deemed to be no one's property, from a churchyard, far from ranking high on the list of moral outrages punishable by law, scarcely ranked at all.

The condition of churchyards was a godsend to the grave-robber, amateur or professional. Operating always in the hours of darkness, he could easily uncover a coffin buried only a few hours before in shallow and uncompacted soil, extract the body, strip it of its shroud or clothing, and stuff it in a sack to cart or carry it away, undiscovered. The amateurs, however – mostly enthusiastic young students – did not develop the sophisticated operating methods of the later professionals, whose natural cunning was soon to make grave-robbing into a business of teamwork and expertise. The amateur effort was often a story of botched jobs and nightmare incompetence. The amateurs rarely attempted to conceal their activities, leaving opened coffins and heaps of soil for all to see, and thus provoked public outrage sooner than would have been the case if professionals, anxious to protect their own interests, had applied their craftiness to the business from the start.

By 1725 the practice of robbing graves by medical

students had already grown to such an extent, especially in Scotland, as to cause public disquiet. Threats were made against anatomists, and Dr Monro's windows in Edinburgh were broken by a mob. The College of Surgeons there, anxious to protect its growing reputation, protested against the violation of churchyards, and had a clause inserted in the indenture of apprentices forbidding them to rob graves. Cambridge University's medical school had found a similar self-denying ordinance necessary some years earlier. Nevertheless, it seems a safe assumption that many students in Scotland, at least, were able to pay for their courses in anatomy by supplying corpses instead of cash; perhaps more so in Glasgow than in Edinburgh, for Glasgow was able to rival the capital by offering tuition at lower fees.

In London, William Cheselden, physician to Queen Anne and Isaac Newton among others, was called to account by the Company of Barber-Surgeons in 1714 for procuring 'the Dead bodies of Malefactors from the place of execution' and dissecting them 'at his own house, as well as during the Company's Publick Lectures as at other times without the leave of the Governors and contrary to the Company's By law in that behalf. By which means it became more difficult for the Beadles to bring away the Company's Bodies and likewise drew away the members of this Company and others from the Public Dissections and Lectures at the Hall.' Cheselden was let off with a reproof, but the incident shows the possessiveness which existed over the few corpses that were legally available, and the growing difficulty in obtaining them is indicated by the fact that in the previous year the Barber-Surgeons had found it necessary to send a clerk to the Secretary of War for a military guard to protect those bringing the next bodies from Tyburn.

After its separation from the barbers, the Surgeons' Company soon ceased to perform dissections on its own premises. The hospital surgeons came to dominate the teaching of anatomy, and the Surgeons' Company actually had to pay students to attend its lectures at one stage. Thereafter Surgeons' Hall acted as a receiving house for executed criminals. Formal incisions were made on the bodies to satisfy the terms of the charter, and the bodies were then distributed to the teaching hospitals.

The intellectual dilemma lay in recognizing the fact that if science was to advance the treatment of disease, the study of human anatomy must go on; whilst also respecting the almost universal Christian faith at that time in literal resurrection of the material body. There was no possible compromise. The doctors naturally gave priority to their research; the public to their religious convictions, reinforced by their justified indignation that it was the poor who were being victimized, as always.

In 1636, the Professor of Medicine at Aberdeen, William Gordon, petitioned not only for the bodies of executed criminals, but also for those of the poor who died in hospitals and 'abortive bairns, foundlings; or of those of no qualitie, who has died of thare diseases, and has few friends or acquaintance that can tak exception.'[1] One defender of the practice of dissection, Bernard de Mandeville, stated bluntly that, even if the relatives of victims felt defiled 'the Dishonour would seldom reach beyond the Scum of the People'.

The leading positions of the medical schools in the chief cities – London and Edinburgh, Glasgow and Dublin – as well as the fame of their surgeons and teachers, all helped the activities of the amateur body-snatchers to become constant topics in the national press, so that their exploits became matters of widespread outrage and familiar gossip. But provincial practice, too, required subjects for anatomists. Although there were no properly organized and recognized provincial schools of anatomy in England at this time except at the universities of Oxford and Cambridge, enterprising medical practitioners at the hospitals would give lectures to their apprentices on the subject, whenever they could get hold of bodies, so that a local tradition grew up and often formed the basis of a proper medical school later on. The first official provincial school of anatomy apart from Oxford and Cambridge was founded in 1814 in Bridge Street, Manchester, by Joseph Jordan, who had twelve students at the time. It was recognized by the Royal College of Surgeons in 1821.

There were varying claims as to the number of cadavers required each year by the country's growing number of students. Some anatomy professors were apt to suggest that no person ought to be let loose on the public as a qualified surgeon before he had dissected at least three corpses. Others were more modest, saying that one corpse was sufficient. But whatever the optimum requirement might be, it could certainly not be met legally from the gallows alone. In practice the dearth of cadavers necessitated a number of students gathering round a table to share the same corpse.

Surgeons in some provincial towns were able to acquire the bodies of executed criminals after the local assizes, but all depended to some extent on local body-snatching expeditions and thus fuelled public wrath. In Leeds, doctors were occasionally granted the bodies of criminals executed after the York Assizes, but doctors also sought the corpses of the unmourned dead from other Yorkshire towns, as well as from the Infirmary, and asked also for the bodies of those who failed to recover in the 'House of Recovery' – the fever hospital. Bristol anatomists also had access to executed criminals. Neither Leeds nor Bristol possessed recognized medical schools, however, until the 1830s.

There are many hair-raising stories of medical students' exploits in obtaining subjects for their professors.[2] They were prepared to take risks to obtain human subjects rather than be reduced to dissecting dogs, monkeys and other animals, which taught them nothing that had not been known for centuries. Two students reputedly dug up the body of a former innkeeper at Leven and unknowingly took it to the very inn he had kept, where they intended to spend the night before returning to Edinburgh with their booty across the Firth of Forth. But the rifled grave was discovered sooner than they had anticipated, and when two constables came to the inn making enquiries, the students fled. The innkeeper's widow found her husband in bed several days after she had seen him buried.

Two students from Bristol Infirmary cut off the head of a negro in the hospital mortuary one night and carried it off towards the lodgings of Francis Cheyne Bowles, who gave private anatomy lessons to eager students without charge, and had promised a demonstration of the brain. On the way there, however, the students dropped the head, and were unable to find it in the dark. Anxious not to be found out, and not wanting to use a light for fear of alerting the watch, they linked arms and slowly walked back and forth over the ground until, after an hour, one of their feet struck the elusive head, which had rolled some distance from where they had dropped it.[3]

In London, the body of the notorious criminal Jonathan Wild – a buckle-maker who had failed to make ends meet and turned to a life of crime – was dug up from St Pancras churchyard in 1725, a few days after his execution at Tyburn, and it was generally assumed that surgeons or their students were responsible.

At York in 1739, the body of an even more famous villain was stolen. In April of that year, Dick Turpin was hanged for horse-stealing and buried in St George's churchyard. Next morning, the body was actually seen being carried away, and a crowd of people, suspecting where it had gone, went in search and found the corpse in the garden of one of the city's surgeons. Carrying it back to the churchyard, they buried Turpin again, covering the body with quicklime to ensure that it would be unsuitable for dissection if the robbers tried again.[4] This practice of hastening decay was not uncommon, but the Church frowned on it for the same reason that the public abhorred dissection – it precluded material resurrection of the body on Judgment Day.

Efforts by friends and relatives to prevent executed criminals from getting into the hands of the surgeons were frequent, and sometimes violent. Consequently executioners, whose job it was to assist beadles in delivering such bodies to dissecting rooms, were often at considerable risk. The accounts of the Worshipful Company of Barber-Surgeons record annual Christmas boxes to executioners, often receipted with the illiterate hangmen's marks, although the signature in 1730 of 'John Hooper Executioner', testifies to his pride in his calling, on the occasion of a gift of seven shillings and sixpence for his year's trouble on the surgeons' behalf.

Hooper was called before the Court of Aldermen shortly before his retirement, however, accused of selling bodies of hanged men to *private* surgeons, when they were supposed to be reserved for the Barber-Surgeons' Company. Competition for bodies between the private teachers of anatomy, the Company of Physicians and the Barber-Surgeons not only aggravated the shortage of corpses for dissection, but also increased the chaos at public executions when the public frequently rioted to prevent *any* surgeon from getting his hands on the victims. An entry in the Barber-Surgeons' annals for 18 December 1741 reads: 'Ordered that the High Constable of Holburne be allowed Ten shillings and sixpence as his ffee for every body that shall be brought from Tyburne and delivered at this Company's Hall and for his aiding and assisting the Company's Beadles therein and not otherwise.'

One eye-witness of the public hangings at Tyburn was surprised to see the populace, in full view of a number of peace officers, 'fall to hauling and pulling the carcases with so much earnestness as to occasion several warm encounters and broken heads. These, I was told, were the friends of the persons executed, or such as, for the sake of tumult, chose to appear so, and some persons sent by private surgeons to obtain bodies for dissection.'[5]

A seventeen-year-old victim of the gallows in 1740, William Duell, was conveyed to the surgeons' dissecting room and laid on a table in preparation for cutting him up when, 'to the great astonishment of the surgeons and assistants', he was heard to groan, and being revived, he was transported for life instead of being subjected to a second hanging. Such recoveries from execution were not uncommon in the days when death by hanging consisted of being strangled at the end of a rope rather than having the neck dislocated by means of the long drop.

The body of 'Long Jack', a well-known vagabond, was returned to its grave by the same men who stole it. Long Jack committed suicide by cutting his throat in 1750, and in accordance with the custom of those days was buried at a cross-roads, at the eastern outskirts of Bristol. Two local surgeons, Abraham Ludlow and his

son, decided to dig the body up, and did so with the
help of two other men, getting the corpse to Mr
Ludlow's house, where they laid it on a table in the back
parlour to await their attention in the morning.
Unfortunately, a maidservant was first to enter the
room, and she ran screaming into the road when she
saw Long Jack lying there with his throat cut. The news
spread rapidly, and some local men threatened
vengeance if they should find the vagabond's grave
empty, but by the time they investigated the alarmed
doctors had managed to put the body back.[6]

In 1768 the Professor of Anatomy at Cambridge
University baulked at dissecting a body which had been
delivered to his table, and had it hastily reburied, after it
had been recognized as Laurence Sterne, the clergyman
and celebrated author of *Tristram Shandy*. The story is
not well authenticated, but the legend is that
body-snatchers – doubtless amateurs – stole the
reverend gentleman from the churchyard of St George
in Hanover Square, London. One version has it that the
professor had already begun the dissection when a
student and former friend of Sterne's recognized the
face and fainted.[7]

One of the earliest recorded indictments for
body-snatching in England was in 1777, when two men
were convicted of removing the body of Mrs Jane
Sainsbury from her grave in the churchyard of St
George the Martyr in London's Queen Square. A few
years later, a man was whipped for stealing another
body from the same churchyard; and a grave-digger
was publicly whipped through the streets of London for
taking the body of a woman from a graveyard in
Wakefield Street.

The grave-digger of St George's in Bloomsbury, and a
woman accomplice, both convicted of stealing a corpse,
were sentenced to a term of imprisonment and were

'whipped twice on their bare backs from the end of King's Gate Street, Holborn, to Dyot Street, St Giles.' It is not clear under what law any of these punishments were meted out, unless clothes and/or coffin fittings were stolen as well.

In 1794, the corpse of a former porter of the Archbishop of Canterbury was among bodies dug up from a graveyard in Paradise Row (now Old Paradise Road) only a few yards from Lambeth Palace, and several bodies were found in a house at Stepney which was used by body-snatchers as a storage depot for corpses prior to sale and distribution. *The Times* called for the death penalty for robbing churchyards, and urged Archbishop Moore to introduce a Bill, but to no avail. Even the Church, not given to pussy-footedness in advocating harsh laws, considered this proposal a bit extreme.

It was in Scotland where fierce opposition to dissection grew soonest and loudest. In March 1742, the corpse of one Alexander Baxter, which had been buried in Edinburgh's West Kirkyard, was found lying in an empty house adjoining the premises of a surgeon, Martin Eccles. An outraged mob soon gathered and did much damage to Eccles' and other surgeons' houses, after seizing the Portsburgh drum, and beating to arms 'down the Cowgate to the foot of Niddery's wynd, till the drum was taken away from them by a party of the city-guard'.[8] It was essential, to maintain public order, that Eccles and some of his students be arrested and charged with grave-robbing, but the charges were duly dropped for lack of proof.

A few days later, the frustrated mob grasped at a rumour that one of the beadles of the West Kirk, named George Haldane, was involved in body-snatching, and his house was burnt down during riots which lasted all night. An account of this affair in the *Scots Magazine*

contains the earliest known use of the word 'resurrection' in connection with body-snatching, referring to
the nicknaming of the beadle's house as 'resurrection
hall'. One might have thought it blasphemous, but the
word came to be generally accepted everywhere,
although 'sack-em-up men' was another popular term,
as well as 'body-snatchers'.[9]

Not long afterwards, the city guard at Edinburgh's
Potterow Port, not far from Surgeons' Hall, stopped a
gardener who was carrying a sack, and discovered in it
the body of a child found later to have been Gaston
Johnson, buried at Pentland kirkyard a week before.
The gardener, John Samuel from Grangegateside, was
publicly whipped through the streets of the town and
banished from Scotland for seven years.[10]

Another gardener, Peter Richardson, had his house at
Inveresk burnt down on suspicion of body-snatching,
and at Glasgow in 1749 there were serious riots when
college students were suspected – no doubt correctly – of
stealing corpses from one of the city's kirkyards. The
angry mob was eventually dispersed when the militia
was called out, but not before several people had been
injured and windows of the university broken.

Riots against doctors were also occurring in the United
States. A Dr Shippen of Philadelphia defended himself
against an angry mob by explaining that the bodies he
dissected were suicides or victims of the hangman,
except, he added unwisely, 'now and then one from the
Potter's Field'. And in 1788 a mob broke into the dissecting room of the New York Hospital and displayed
several heads and limbs to public view at the windows.
The riot continued for two days, and was only suppressed by the civil and military authorities at the cost of
five deaths and several casualties.

In 1752 in Scotland, a more ominous event had occurred which ought to have alerted the government of

the day to the urgent need for legislation. Two Edinburgh women, Helen Torrence and Jean Waldie, met a woman named Johnston with her young son John, and invited her to come home with them for a drink, leaving the boy, who was eight or nine years old, playing in the street. While the mother was in Torrence's house enjoying her drink, Waldie went out to find the boy, and took him back to her own rooms, immediately above Torrence's, where she suffocated him with bedclothes. The two women later took the body to a surgeon and were offered two shillings for it. Haggling over the price, they got it raised by ten pence, and the one who carried it got an extra six pence. After four days, the body was found 'with evident marks of its having been in the surgeons' hands'.

Both women were tried and found guilty of murder, for which they were sentenced to death. It turned out that they were nursing women who had promised the surgeon the body of a sick infant whom they confidently expected to die within a few days, but when he unexpectedly recovered, they hit on the idea of substituting a different child. Waldie claimed that the boy had been accidentally smothered in her coats as she took him home, and counsel for the defence argued that, as selling a dead body was not a crime at all, they should be sentenced only for the lesser offence of kidnapping. Torrence tried to evade the death penalty by pleading that she was pregnant – a claim that was soon disproved.

The two women were hanged in Edinburgh's Grassmarket, less than a year after an Act was passed which decreed that *all* executed murderers were to be either publicly dissected or hung in chains.[11] The new law was introduced not in the spirit of aid to medical research (although the government doubtless expected that it would go some way towards satisfying the doctors' demands for more corpses), but as an additional punishment. With so many capital crimes against property now on the statute book, it was thought desirable to distinguish murder with a peculiarly horrific penalty. The preamble to the 'Act for Preventing the horrid Crime of Murder' (25 Geo. II) asserted that 'It is become necessary that some further Terror and peculiar Mark of Infamy be added to the Punishment.'

Some criminals, faced with such a choice of evils, preferred the thought of dissection, as it would be over relatively soon after death. Bodies hanging in chains sometimes remained on gibbets for years: black masses of putrefying flesh half eaten by birds and insects. The Postmaster General in 1753 (the Earl of Leicester) received an anonymous letter after the body of one criminal was hung in chains instead of being dissected, as had originally been ordered: 'My lord, I find it was by your orders that Mr Stockdale was hung in chains. Now, if you don't order him to be taken down, I will set fire to your house, and blow your brains out the first opportunity.' (The threat was not carried out, though the late Mr Stockdale remained where he was.)

Most people, however, undoubtedly had the more common horror of the surgeon's table, like the Smithfield butcher Vincent Davis, who stabbed his wife to death in 1725. When the constables came to arrest him, he confessed immediately, saying: 'I have killed the best wife in the world, and I am certain of being hanged, but for God's sake, don't let me be anatomised.' His friends managed to protect him from the surgeons, and buried him at Clerkenwell.

Likewise Richard Tobin, who worked at the Globe Tavern in Hatton Garden, wrote to his master when he was condemned to death for stealing a peruke in 1739: ' ... my Freinds is very Poor, and my Mother is very sick, and I am to die next Wednesday Morning ... so I hope you will take it into Consideration of my poor Body, consedar if it was your own Cace, you would be willing to have your Body saved from the Surgeons ... '[12]

The new Murder Act also prescribed a penalty of seven years' transportation for attempting to rescue a body on its way from gallows to Surgeons' Hall, but the opposition of the poor was too powerful and deep-seated, and they could not be deterred from attempting to save friends and relations from the ignominy of the scalpel. Otherwise brave men shrank from the thought of it. When one of Wellington's army commanders, Sir William Myers, was dying of his wounds in the Peninsular War, he said to the regimental surgeon: 'I have, I confess it, a prejudice against being opened of which I am ashamed but which I cannot get the better of. Promise me that it shall not be done.' The general had, of course, no scruples about committing to army surgeons the bodies of his men, who might have had similar prejudices. Class distinction punctuates the public pronouncements of doctors, politicians and others on the subject throughout its history.

Nor were surgeons themselves immune to the fear of ending up under the knives of their colleagues. Robert Southey, whose life was contemporaneous with the most active period of body-snatching, wrote a prophetic poem in 1796 called 'The Surgeon's Warning', in which a former anatomist's apprentices succeed in stealing his body for dissection despite all his precautions before his death:

> And all night long let three stout men
>   The vestry watch within;
> To each man give a gallon of beer,
>   And a keg of Holland's gin;

> Powder and ball and ball and blunderbuss,
>   To save me if he can,
> And eke five guineas if he shoot
>   A Resurrection Man.
>
> And let them watch me for three weeks,
>   My wretched corpse to save,
> For then I think that I may stink
>   Enough to rest in my grave.

The poem hints at the various measures which were by then beginning to be taken by private individuals to protect their newly buried dead from the resurrection men. Armed guards were sometimes hired to watch churchyards by night, and spring-guns were occasionally set near new graves. Students were sometimes injured by these, and one was killed in Glasgow's Blackfriars kirkyard. In Edinburgh, a man had a crude land-mine placed in his daughter's grave. Another method, and generally a more effective one, was to have a colossal slab of stone lowered on to a fresh grave until the danger of exhumation was past. At Kemnay, near Aberdeen, they used a slab of granite six feet long and nearly a foot thick, lowering it with block-and-tackle on to the grave, leaving it there for as long as was thought necessary, then moving it to the next new grave that required it.

Amateur body-snatchers who were caught were liable to be badly beaten or kicked, thrown into rivers, or worse. Peter Harkan, an anatomy demonstrator in Dublin, was caught by watchmen climbing over the wall of the hospital burial ground. Whilst they pulled him by his legs from one side, his students pulled him by his arms from the other, and he never fully recovered from the injuries he received.

Churchyards on the northern bank of the Firth of Forth were favourite haunts of students from Edinburgh. Rowing a body across in a boat was quieter and less likely to be detected than transporting it by road. The surgeon Robert Liston, whose father was the minister at Ecclesmachan, not far from Edinburgh, led body-snatching expeditions himself as a student. There is a story that he and his colleagues stole the corpse of a young sailor from the kirkyard at Rosyth, just across the Firth, almost from under the nose of the victim's former fiancée, who saw them rowing away after finding the empty grave of her loved one.

Another tale concerning Liston's excursions across the water is that he and a companion lifted a corpse from Culross and dumped it behind a hedge, in a sack, whilst they went for refreshment in a local inn. They were sitting drinking there when a cry of 'Ship ahoy!' was heard outside, and a drunken sailor burst in with their sack on his shoulder. He was the brother of the woman who kept the inn and, dropping the sack on the floor, he started to cut the rope that tied it, saying, 'If it ain't something good, rot them chaps there that stole it!' He had been dozing behind the hedge when the unsuspecting and now dumbfounded students dumped their load almost on top of him. When the neck of the sack fell open to reveal the head of a dead man, brother and sister alike fled, and Liston and his colleague successfully made off with their prize.

The surgeons and extramural anatomy lecturers of Edinburgh had their premises in Surgeons' Square, close to the old Infirmary near the Cowgate. The hospital had its own burial ground for the unclaimed dead, and this was very convenient for the Square's students, but of course was totally inadequate for all their needs. The two leading lecturers when Liston first came on the scene as a lecturer himself were Doctors Monro and Barclay, who had established territorial rights between themselves to the most convenient and productive graveyards in the vicinity, but Liston did not respect either of their happy hunting grounds, and sought subjects wherever he pleased. He was to become famous many years after these events as the first surgeon in Europe to carry out an operation on an anaesthetized patient, when he amputated one of Frederick Churchill's legs at University College Hospital, London, in December 1846, using ether.

In England and Scotland, the demand for bodies so far outstripped the capabilities of both students and early professionals to keep pace with it, that an import trade started from France and Ireland, where bodies were cheap and plentiful. Corpses could be bought from Irish body-snatchers for ten shillings each in the early days. Glasgow was the main clearing-house for corpses imported from Ireland, but such cargoes were also received at the ports of London, Liverpool, Bristol and Aberdeen, among others. Liverpool was usually the destination for exports from Dublin, because the sea-crossing was shorter and bodies were less likely to rot during the voyage. Ships delayed by bad weather from entering port were liable to be detected by their stench, and dead bodies found on docked vessels were usually buried at sea. Shippers hoped to escape detection by labelling their crates or casks 'fish' or 'apples' or 'glue'.

A terrible stench from a shed at Glasgow's Broomielaw led to the discovery of putrefying corpses which had been sent to Scotland by Irish medical students, documented as a cargo of cotton and linen rags, and addressed to a merchant in Jamaica Street. One Scottish surgeon, named Rae and nicknamed 'the Captain', started a new career by packing exhumed corpses and shipping them across the Irish Sea in steamboats.

Cargoes of bodies landed at the country's leading ports were intended for medical schools in various towns and cities to which they had to be transported, more often than not, by road. How often well-bred and unsuspecting passengers in coaches between, say, London and Cambridge, travelled in the company of dead bodies in crates is only to be guessed at, but at Carlisle, where coaches stopped for the night on the journey between Liverpool and Glasgow, the coroner became well known for his frequent non-committal verdict, 'Found dead in a box'.

Medical students looked out for funerals in their districts, and were particularly keen, naturally enough, to dig up the bodies of those who had died of unusual and interesting diseases. There was also much interest in the physically malformed. The corpse of a dwarf, Alexander Ross, who was nicknamed 'Shotty', was stolen from the kirkyard at Dalmaik, but rescued by angry locals before it could be dissected.

'How long will a man lie i' the earth ere he rot?' Hamlet asks the grave-digger, and gets the answer: 'I' faith, if he be not rotten before he die ... he will last you some eight year or nine year ... ' Shakespeare was, on this occasion at least, optimistic, but doctors acquired the remains of another dwarf, David Ritchie, ten years after his burial at Peebles, so it is said, though what state he was in by that time one hesitates to imagine. The skeleton was obviously the object of interest.

The great John Hunter acquired the body of Charles Byrne, or O'Brien, an Irish circus giant who died in 1783 at the age of twenty-two, by bribing the men who had promised Byrne that they would put him in a lead coffin and bury him at sea. Hunter preserved the skeleton and it remains to this day a prominent exhibit in a glass case in the Hunterian Museum of the Royal College of Surgeons.

A doctor at Bristol Infirmary made a casual note in June 1870: 'Assisted by an Infirmary patient, dug up a

child with a remarkably large Hydrocephalus from St
James's Churchyard.'[13] Such nonchalant dealing with
the deceased was common. One doctor is said to have
made a practice of digging up his own former patients,
and on one occasion, having secured the body of a
youth, met the mother while returning home. She was
on her way to the churchyard to see that her son's grave
had not been disturbed. The doctor assured her that it
was all right, as he had just come from there, and he
offered her a lift home in his gig, which she gratefully
accepted, oblivious to the fact that her son's corpse was
stuffed under her seat.

It was not unknown for intrepid medical students to
dress a corpse in ordinary day clothes, taken along for
the purpose, and 'walk' it through the streets, one
student on either side with an arm through the
subject's. Anyone who saw them would take little
notice in the early days, assuming it was merely another
student being taken home sick or drunk by his mates.

As the traffic in corpses gathered momentum,
though, the public became more suspicious and
increasingly outraged. The inflamed mood of the
Glasgow population is well illustrated by the case of an
imaginative citizen who looked through the shop
window of George Provand, an oil and colour
merchant, and thought he saw blood and severed
heads. An angry crowd soon gathered as the false
witness told his story, and the innocent merchant's
premises were ransacked. One of the ringleaders of this
riot was subsequently whipped through the streets.

In Aberdeen, the minutes of the Medico-Chirurgical
Society record several instances of grave-robbing by its
students, who were usually called before the Procurator
Fiscal and fined. The secretary of the society in 1801,
Charles Jameson, was himself charged with disinterring
the corpse of a miller, James Marr, from its grave in the

hospital burial ground. In 1805, four students dug up a corpse from the Old Town kirkyard for dissection by their professor, Dr Skene, and only a fortnight afterwards, four others exhumed a female corpse from the same kirkyard for dissection by the same doctor.

In April 1801, law officers were called to quell a riot at a building in Wych Street in London, after a crowd had been drawn to the site by a rumour that surgeons dissected bodies there. Flesh had been buried in the cellar and was giving off a terrible stench, and the noisy demonstrators had put two and two together and made five, assuming that the doctors, whose instruments were found on the premises, had murdered their subjects. There was no evidence to support this assumption, and the remains found were reburied in St Clement Dane's churchyard.

As time went on, punishments were increased in line with the growing public clamour for protection of the dead, and medical students began to be harassed and threatened in the streets. Three apprentice surgeons from Keith were imprisoned for four months in 1817 for stealing the body of John Bremner from the cemetery at Aberdeen. By this time, however, professional body-snatchers were everywhere in Britain relieving students of the burden of responsibility for quarrying their own raw materials.

Chapter III: Opportunities for Specialists

'Father,' said young Jerry, as they walked along, taking care to keep at arm's length and to have the stool well between them, 'what's a Resurrection Man?'

Mr Cruncher came to a stop on the pavement before he answered, 'How should I know?'

'I thought you knowed everything, father,' said the artless boy.

'Hem! Well,' returned Mr Cruncher, going on again, and lifting off his hat to give his spikes free play, 'he's a tradesman.'

'What's his goods, father?' asked the brisk young Jerry.

'His goods,' said Mr Cruncher, after turning it over in his mind, 'is a branch of Scientific goods.'

'Persons' bodies, ain't it, father?' asked the lively boy.

'I believe it is something of that sort,' said Mr Cruncher.

'Oh father, I should so like to be a Resurrection Man when I'm quite growed up!'

Charles Dickens
A Tale of Two Cities, 1859

Men with an eye for the main chance soon became aware, through rumours, riots and press reports, that here was an opportunity they could not afford to miss. For the sake of a bit of nocturnal gardening, as it were, they could supplement their incomes by helping to satisfy the anatomists' demand for corpses, and they

would scarcely be breaking the law. It seemed too good
to be true. At first, they took on work as casual
labourers, doing a job when an opportunity presented
itself and, as itinerant salesmen, disposing of a body
here and a body there. But as time went on, and the
demand for subjects continued to increase, there were
those who made a speciality of body-snatching, and
turned the robbing of graves into a profession,
encouraged – and sometimes virtually employed – by
the leading teachers of anatomy, who were out of
business themselves if they had no corpses.

The professionals were referred to as 'grabs' in
underworld parlance, and what they grabbed was not
usually called a body, or a corpse, or a subject, but a
'thing'. They brought a degree of finesse to their work
that was beyond the amateurs who only wanted bodies
as easily as they could get them, and were not trying to
protect a trade. No shattered coffins and open graves
were left to provoke local communities into defensive
action, the professionals taking care to put back empty
coffins in the graves and restore the soil and turf so that,
nothing being suspected, the same churchyards could
safely be visited again. When a woman died at Great
Yarmouth in 1827, desiring to be buried with her
husband, the grave-diggers opened the grave only to
find it empty. There was panic among the local
population, especially when further investigation
revealed that many other graves in the churchyard were
empty, too. Three men – William and Robert Barber and
Thomas Smith – were arrested and charged in
connection with these exhumations. The Barbers
turned King's Evidence, and described how they had
dug up the twenty-odd bodies and sent them to
London by wagon. The unfortunate Smith got six
months.[1] Similarly, when body-snatchers were disturbed at their work in the graveyard at Kirkmichael,

near Ayr, in 1829, searches revealed that no less than twenty-two bodies were missing from their graves.

Working with shovels, crowbars, pick-axes, screw-drivers, ropes and sacks, two men working by the light of an oil-lamp, with another to keep watch, could quickly and quietly unearth a coffin, unscrew the lid, extract the corpse and strip it, putting the shroud or clothing back in the coffin, which they then buried again, leaving the churchyard virtually as they had found it, except for the missing resident.

Excavated soil was usually piled on sacks or canvas sheets so that it could be tipped back – another economical ruse, saving time and labour in shovelling. One professional resurrectionist claimed to have raised a body in a quarter of an hour. Another said he had taken two bodies from separate graves and restored the coffins and the soil, all within an hour and a half.

Did body-snatchers spirit away the corpse of Henry Trigg from Stevenage, one wonders? A grocer and churchwarden, he died in 1724 leaving an odd instruction in his will that he committed his body 'to the West end of my Hovel to be decently laid there upon a floor erected by my Executor, upon the purloyne, for the same purpose; nothing doubting but at the general Resurrection I shall receive the same again by the mighty power of God.' And sure enough, his coffin was placed in the rafters of his barn and remained there for two and a half centuries attracting the curious, whilst the former grocer's shop became the Castle Inn and then a bank. But the coffin was eventually found to be empty, and perhaps had been so within a few days of being placed there, an open temptation to the local body-snatchers to effect Mr Trigg's resurrection rather sooner than he had anticipated and send him packing down the Great North Road.[2]

Since bodies could not be sold in the middle of the

night, the usual practice was to stuff corpses into sacks and leave them in some convenient but well-hidden spot, returning to collect them the next day. This could sometimes have unexpected results. In February 1809, the naked body of Mrs Janet Spark was washed up on the coast at Nigg Bay, near Aberdeen. Mrs Spark, ninety years old when she died, the widow of an Aberdeen shipmaster and step-mother of the Treasurer of Aberdeen Royal Infirmary, had been buried in St Fittick's kirkyard, three days before Christmas. The body-snatchers who dug her up, with the doctors at the city's Marischal College in mind as their customers, were disturbed at their work, and although they got away from the kirkyard with the corpse, they thought it wiser not to ferry it across the Dee that night, so they buried it in a sand bank. They did not foresee the storm that blew up, washing away both the bank and the remains of Mrs Spark.

The resurrection men were sometimes allowed to store their night's gleanings in the outhouses of hospitals prior to negotiation. The doorkeepers or assistants who had been authorized to deal with the resurrection men on behalf of the anatomists (for these distinguished surgeons and professors did not usually want to meet the body-snatchers face to face) would receive the corpses and deposit them in cold cellars, the longer to preserve them in a suitable condition for dissection.

The doctors were not always fussy about having *whole* bodies. They sometimes sought *parts* of bodies which they knew to be diseased, having treated the victims before their deaths, and knowing them to be eminently suitable for discourses on morbid anatomy. They would occasionally purchase 'opened' bodies (those which had been operated on or subjected to post-mortem examinations) when they were short of subjects, but they paid less for these inferior specimens.

The body-snatchers also discovered a useful by-product of their trade with the anatomists. They could sell good teeth to dentists. Fashionable people then wanted their dentures made of real teeth. When Professor Macartney of Trinity College, Dublin, argued against organizing guards on the graves in Bully's Acre burial ground, and thus interfering with the progress of anatomy, he pointed out that many of the very people who were loudest in their protests against body-snatching had mouths full of teeth which had been buried in that very place.

The growing experience of the resurrection men led to greater sophistication of method. Professionals soon devised means of getting bodies out of graves without digging up the coffins. All they had to do was dig down to the wider head end of the coffin lid, get a crowbar under it, and lever it upward until it split across, the weight of the soil holding the rest firmly in place. Then they could pull the body out, using a rope or hook. 'In the disinterment of bodies,' Frederick Lonsdale wrote in his biography of Robert Knox, 'considerable force was required, and this was mainly exerted round the neck by means of a cord and other appliances. Now, withdrawing the contents of a coffin by a narrow aperture was by no means an easy process, particularly at dead of night and whilst the actors were in a state of trepidation: a jerking movement is said to have been more effective than violent dragging.'

The crack of splitting wood was obviously a risky noise, but the sound could be muffled with sacking, and this method had the advantage of a considerable saving in time and labour. One ingenious variation on this system was the use of a long iron 'corkscrew'. When the lid of a coffin was exposed at the head end, this tool could be screwed through the lid and then heaved up until the lid split open. Part of such a tool is preserved as the lychgate bolt at the church of Salcombe Regis in Devon, a quiet village churchyard once susceptible to visits from body-snatchers.

When paupers' graves were chosen, it was still necessary to remove coffins whole, because they were buried on top of one another. Although this entailed much extra work, it could be profitable in a busy town churchyard, where common graves often contained many coffins buried in a short period, for the pits were dug and then left open until they had been filled with coffins.

Fanciful methods were sometimes attributed to body-snatchers to account for the disappearance of corpses from apparently undisturbed graves. The *Lancet* went on record in its first weeks of existence, in 1823, as believing that resurrectionists approached a coffin via a tunnel, excavated at a sloping angle from some yards away, so that the surface of the grave was left untouched. But the experts in the trade pointed out that such a method would have been much harder work, taking a great deal longer than digging through the soft and loose soil only recently replaced on the grave itself after the funeral. The professionals simply took good care to hide their tracks, that was all.

Body-snatchers, like grave-diggers, were prone to drunkenness because of the nature of their work. In Scotland, whisky was cheap, and what the English lacked in whisky they made up for in gin. Some resurrection men who resisted the temptation to spend their ill-gotten gains on fortifying themselves for the next job made tidy sums of money. One of them opened a hotel in Margate on the proceeds of several years as a body-snatcher.

Professional resurrectionists spent much of their time in the daylight hours spying on funerals, observing the sites of newly made graves, and bribing sextons and undertakers. The latter could often be persuaded to put weak fastenings on coffins, and grave-diggers would, for a consideration, mark fresh graves, or bury coffins in shallow soil to make the job easier. This put temptation in the way of grave-diggers themselves, of course, the more enterprising among them seeing no reason why they should not make all the profit themselves. Geordie Mill, a grave-digger at the parish burial ground called the 'howff', was a notorious seller of corpses in Dundee. Another well-known operator, supplying the doctors in Aberdeen, was 'resurrectionist Marr', who was a grave-digger at Newhills. All the grave-digger/ resurrectionist had to do was to wait until the last of the mourners had departed after a funeral, then unscrew the coffin lid and remove the corpse before burying the box in the normal way. He would usually cover the body with shallow soil until it was dark, when he could return and carry it away from the churchyard.

Spies also helped to get round the dangers of spring-guns and other booby-traps set for the grave-robbers, by carefully observing the positions of trip-wires, so that the weapons could be avoided or removed first and then replaced. Thus, although there were occasional injuries from such traps, they were generally ineffective in deterring the resurrection men. Indeed, there is a story that one expert lifted seven bodies out of a paupers' grave protected by a spring-gun.

Heightening of churchyard walls, or surmounting them with iron railings, also proved ineffective. There was nothing to stop the resurrection men from carrying ladders with them if necessary. The simplest methods of protection were often the most effective. A huge slab of stone placed on top of a new grave served well enough, because body-snatchers never worked in groups large enough to be able to move it, even if they considered it worth the time and effort. The kirkyard at St Fittick near Aberdeen was a favourite haunt of body-snatchers until the superintendent of work at Aberdeen harbour provided a large block of dressed granite which was lowered on to the lid of a coffin before the grave was filled in with soil. This had the desired effect on any grave privileged to receive it, but the idea that the robbers would be deterred by uncertainty as to whether they were going to spend an hour digging only to reach an impassable obstacle clearly proved optimistic, for this parish subsequently found it necessary, as did so many others, to erect a watch-house.

One or two of these stone slabs survive in the churchyards where they were used, for instance at Pannal, North Yorkshire, where the so-called Resurrection Stone, over a ton in weight, used to be hired out at a guinea a fortnight. There are also many iron *mort-safes*, later refinements of the same principle, which were particularly popular in Scotland. 'The iron cage or safe is a Scotch invention which we have lately seen at Glasgow,' wrote a correspondent to the *Quarterly Review*, 'where it has been in use between two and three years ... The price paid for this apparatus is a shilling a day.'[3] One of the designers of an iron mort-safe was a farmer of Fintry, Peter Brownie, who had been a resurrectionist himself, but was converted to Quakerism and then, fully repentant and feeling a bit cut up about his shameful past, no doubt, put his knowledge to good use in thwarting what he had previously exploited.

The mort-safe was a strong and heavy iron grille which was lowered by block-and-tackle into a grave to form a cage round the coffin until the danger of disinterment was past. After a few weeks, the contraption could safely be removed, and was available for the next customer. A mort-safe used at Banchory-Devenick weighed nearly a ton, and is said to have been last used as late as 1854, when body-snatching had been more-or-less eliminated for twenty years. Another huge mort-safe was kept in the churchyard at Colinton, where Robert Louis Stevenson's maternal grandfather, Lewis Balfour, was the parish minister.

Even this method of protecting the dead was not entirely foolproof, however. In 1915 an iron mort-safe was uncovered during digging in the kirkyard at Aberlour, but was found to contain an empty coffin! An enormous mort-safe stands over a grave at Aberfoyle; several remain in Glasgow and Edinburgh, particularly in the latter's Greyfriars churchyard; and in England, a rare example can still be seen in the churchyard at Henham, Essex.

The availability and relative cheapness of iron as a result of the industrial revolution led to occasional burial in iron coffins. Lead coffins had been used, by those who could afford them, for a long time, not for protection from grave-robbers so much as from bodily corruption, on the religious grounds that they would be better prepared for resurrection on Judgment Day. But in 1818 Edward Bridgman, a London undertaker, began to bury those who wished it in iron coffins which had no external screws or hinges. When he attempted thus to bury the wife of a Mr Gilbert of Holborn, however, he was stopped by the authorities and a long legal wrangle ensued. There was fierce opposition to the practice in some quarters because the imperishable material aggravated the already controversial state of crowded city churchyards. The late Mrs Gilbert remained unburied for many weeks, until the Consistory Court made its decision, ruling that Mr Bridgman's iron coffins were permissible. Thereupon, he lost no time in advertising his patent coffins with a grim warning to the public that 'many hundred dead bodies will be dragged from their wooden coffins this winter, for the anatomical lectures (which have just commenced), the articulators, and for those who deal in the dead for the supply of the country practitioner and the Scotch schools.' The only safe coffin, Mr Bridgman assured the public, was his patent wrought-iron one, no more expensive than a wooden one, and superior to lead.

The craftiness and cunning of the professional grave-robbers provoked increasing ingenuity in the grieving and fearful relatives of the newly deceased. In Scotland, stone burial vaults became popular in some places, where coffins could be locked away until a few weeks after death, when they could be safely taken out and buried. Crail, Fintry and Marnoch were among the parishes which built such vaults.

In 1832 Udny, near Aberdeen, responded to the general panic over revelations about the extent of body-snatching by building a circular granite fortress, soon named the 'Round House', in the kirkyard. It was paid for by public subscription, and had a revolving floor inside its doors. A coffin was placed inside, the staging was turned to make room for the next one, and so each coffin made its progress round the building and eventually came back to the doorway. By this time it was thought safe to bury it. The irony is that this elaborate precaution was virtually obsolete by the time it was built, as the Anatomy Act, which became law in August of that year, killed the trade in exhumed corpses.

By far the most widespread precaution throughout Britain was the appointment of night-watchmen, and many parishes built permanent watch huts in their churchyards. These varied from the small stone sentry-box affair like the one remaining at Wanstead, to larger buildings like the one at St John Horselydown,

Bermondsey, now altered and in use as business premises.

Warblington, in Hampshire, built two watch huts, at opposite corners of the churchyard, in aggressive fashion, with thin courses of jagged-edged flints protruding from the walls of flint and brick. At Banchory, near Aberdeen they built a two-storey watchtower containing a bell, which guards could toll to warn others if danger threatened. Banchory-Devenick also had a watch house; and the Calton burial ground in Edinburgh and the churchyards at Kinross, Aberlour and Carmunnock, as well as Morpeth and Doddington in Northumberland, were among the many other places that sought to protect their dead by these means. Those watch huts that survive are now used, more often than not, for storing sextons' tools, and have their windows blocked up.

Sometimes, paid guards would be employed, but more often volunteers from the community would take it in turns to spend nights in these gloomy surroundings. Glasgow had a North Quarter Friendly Churchyard Guard Association with two thousand members. 'I understand,' a correspondent wrote to the *Gentleman's Magazine* in 1826, 'that in Glasgow graves have been watched by people furnished with firearms.' They had indeed, and other weapons were occasionally furnished, too. The watch house at Aberlour had a veritable armoury of muskets and claymores, but the obvious dangers of untrained and undisciplined men using firearms in churchyards, against others who were not committing serious crimes even if caught red-handed – not to mention the possibility of a perfectly innocent citizen being shot on sight by nervous guards – eventually led to the banning of such weapons. In October 1827, a man was killed at Portsmouth when a watchman fired at him on seeing him apparently digging up a body. It turned out that the victim was one of four youths who were playing a practical joke on a friend who was watching a grave, by pretending to be resurrection men.[4]

The system had other weaknesses. The job was obviously very tedious. Most nights, nothing happened, and single guards fell asleep. So it became customary for two or more to keep watch together, sometimes employing passwords when the watch was changed, and being well supplied with tobacco and alcohol to help them keep their vigils in some comfort. But then they tended to get drunk, and Carmunnock, for example, found it necessary to ban alcohol from its watch house in 1828, drawing up regulations for the two-man watch which forbade them from 'getting intoxicated, or leaving the churchyard' between sunset and daybreak. Furthermore, 'No visitor is allowed to enter on any account without the password for the night. They are also prohibited from making any noise or firing guns, except when giving alarm, that any of the inhabitants in such case may turn out to the assistance of the watch.' The less scrupulous guards were open to bribery by the resurrection men.

One London hospital, as keen to receive corpses as any other, but preferably not from its own burial ground, hired a former body-snatcher to guard it. He remained conscientious and incorruptible for some months, but at last succumbed to the temptation of going for a few drinks with his old pals, who then dug up a body they wanted whilst he lay stupefied in his watch hut.

Not that the professional resurrectionists resorted to bribery if they could avoid parting with their money, and they usually could. Courses in anatomy and surgery at the medical schools almost invariably took place during the autumn and winter months, when it was cold in the dissection rooms. The stench would have been unbearable on hot summer days. Thus the demand for corpses was greatest in winter, when it got dark early, so the body-snatchers simply took to visiting churchyards early in the evenings, before the watches came on.

There is a story that Mr Hall Overend, a Sheffield surgeon who later founded the first medical school there, wanted the body of a deformed woman who had died, and tried unsuccessfully to persuade her relatives to part with it. They then quite naturally feared that an attempt might be made to get hold of the body after burial, and prepared to mount a constant watch in the village churchyard after dark. But the surgeon's resurrectionist agents managed to snatch the corpse between the funeral and nightfall, and the unsuspecting relatives spent many nights keeping anxious vigil over an already empty grave. The woman's skeleton duly turned up in the anatomical museum of the Sheffield General Infirmary.

There seemed to be no hiding place from the resurrection men, despite the lengths to which even poor people were prepared to go in order to foil them. A man named John Barnet, who was hanged in Aberdeen in 1818 for burglary, was buried at sea by relatives to keep him safe from the medical sharks at least, but his body was duly washed up at the mouth of the River Don, and they got him anyway.

Above Glenkiln Reservoir, however, west of Dumfries, is the resting place of an eccentric shepherd, John Turner, who laboriously dug out a grave for himself from the solid rock of a hilltop thirteen hundred feet above sea level, so as to be safe from the body-snatchers. And Mary Gibson, a lady of Sutton, Surrey, who died in 1773, ignorant of the fact that no one wanted a corpse after it had been buried for more than about a month, left a bequest in her will to pay for an annual inspection of her grave to ensure that it had not been disturbed.[5]

Some professional resurrection men became very well known in their local areas, and a few achieved wider fame or notoriety. Among the London resurrectionists was Ben Crouch, a one-time prize-fighter, called the 'corpse-king' by some, and leader of a gang which operated in and around the borough of Southwark. He wore good clothes and a profusion of large gold rings, according to author Bransby Cooper. It was he who, after his gradual retirement from the business, had made enough money to enable him to run a small seaside hotel for a time, until his former profession caught up with him and he was reduced to poverty.

The members of Crouch's gang at different times included Bill Harnett and his nephew Jack, Tom Light, Bill Hollis, Jack Hutton and Tom Butler. Hollis had been a grave-digger, and probably lost his job through an informer among the professionals, who naturally resented the private enterprise of amateurs who sold bodies direct to the hospitals. The only qualifications grave-diggers had – accustomed to digging and the handling of corpses – fitted them perfectly to become professional body-snatchers themselves when they lost their jobs, as a great many of them did.

Tom Light – a former 'gentleman's gentleman' – got out of the business after a few years. He was a clumsy worker, and ended up in custody too often, once being caught trying to get three corpses over the wall of a graveyard into Pancras Road, and on another occasion being apprehended carting seven bodies up Holborn Hill in broad daylight. He saw the error of his ways, and became a Methodist.

Another member of the Southwark gang was Joseph Naples, who had served under Nelson at Cape St

Vincent. After his discharge from the navy, Naples got a job as a grave-digger in Spa Fields burial grounds at Clerkenwell, and spent three years there with a profitable sideline in supplying bodies to the medical schools, starting with dead infants and progressing to adults. When he was sacked and sentenced to a term of imprisonment in 1802, Astley Cooper, who was obviously one of his best clients, intervened with the Home Secretary on his behalf, and after his release Naples became a full-time resurrectionist. He and his cronies did business with schools in Edinburgh as well as those in London, generally getting a guinea for a child and four for an adult, though the doctors' agents would reduce the price by half a guinea if any corpse delivered to them had already been opened, for instance by a pathologist to determine the cause of death.

Naples is generally thought to have been the author of a diary, some pages of which survive in the possession of the Royal College of Surgeons.[6] The entry for Wednesday, 2 December 1812, is a fair sample of its contents:

> Met at Mr. Vicker's pub. Rectified our last account. The party sent out me and Ben to St. Thomas's Crib.* Got one adult. Bill and Jack went to Guy's Crib. Got two adults. Took them to St. Thomas's. Came home. Met at St. Thomas's. Me and Jack went to Tottenham. Got four adults. Ben and Bill went to St. Pancras. Got six adults, one small and one foetus. Took the Tottenham lot to Wilson, the St. Pancras lot to Bart's.

The diary lists numbers of bodies obtained, dates,

---

* crib – underworld slang for a burial ground

and how they were disposed of, between November 1811 and December 1812. There are no entries for May, June or July, because there was little demand for bodies at that time during the summer months.[7]

The writer frequently recorded going to 'look out' during the daytime, and occasionally meeting patrols at night or being attacked by dogs. Sometimes he was unable to go out on a job because he or his colleague was drunk:

> '*Wednesday, January 15th, 1812*
> Went to St. Thomas's. Came back, packd up 2 large and 1 small for Edinburgh. At home all Night.
> *Tuesday, January 21st*
> Lookd out. Jack and Butler Drunk as before hindred us of Going Out, at home –
> *Friday, January 24th*
> Met at 11 at night. Met the Patrols. Got 1 Hospital Crib and 6 at Bermondsey, took them to Bartho*m* Sent 3 to the country.'

The entry for 1 April 1812 is curious – 'Party went to the Green. Got 4 adults being the 1 of April the man lay in a new Hat.' J.B. Bailey in the published version read this as 'left us a new Hat', but this reading makes no sense. It seems to me that three of the four adults were women, and the other a man who had been buried only that day by a relative or friend with a sense of humour. The 'Green' was no doubt Bethnal Green, and the subject Jewish.

At the end of the manuscript pages is one on which the diarist wrote out the rules for working out the moon's phases – a full moon could occasionally be a useful ally to the grave-robber, in a very isolated churchyard, but was more often a time to avoid going out for fear of being seen.

The hospitals' own burial grounds, or 'cribs', were not necessarily adjacent to the hospital buildings, and could therefore be raided as freely as other graveyards. St Bartholomew's Hospital burial ground, for instance, was in Seward Street, some distance away. St Thomas's was at the corner of Maze Pond, close to Guy's, whose own burial ground was in Snow's Fields, a little farther away. A recreation ground was eventually made on this site. The London Hospital's burial ground was in the hospital precincts. The last burials took place there around 1860, and the medical school and nurses' home were built on it.

Some of the professionals had part of their training in dealing with death on the battlefields of Europe. Crouch, Butler and Jack Harnett are all said to have followed like hyenas in the wake of the armies in the Peninsular War, reaping the harvest of teeth from dead soldiers. Bransby Cooper alleged that it would not have been beyond them to murder wounded soldiers lying on the battlefields waiting for attention, in order to remove their teeth, not to mention looting their other property.

There were other operators outside the Crouch gang who were technically not resurrection men at all, such as Israel Chapman and Cornelius Bryant, who were a step ahead of the grave-robbers in realizing that 'things' could be obtained before they were buried – sometimes by doing deals with the masters of workhouses, undertakers, or even the relatives of the deceased; sometimes by stealing bodies before funerals took place. In 1826 a man named Joliffe, living at Bethnal Green, tried to bring a charge against two men he alleged had stolen the body of his wife (who had died only that same night), while Mr Joliffe was asleep in the next room. But he was told by the magistrate that there was no law the men had broken unless they had also

taken away some article of clothing or other property –
which, of course, they had not.

Edinburgh had its own celebrities, if that is the word.
Andrew Merrilees, commonly known as 'Merry
Andrew', was a tall, thin and unkempt character who
had been a carter at one time, but falling on hard times,
had turned to body-snatching, inspired by the
graveyard next to which he lived. He is said to have
drunk a bottle of whisky a day, and was supposed by
some to be mentally deficient, but he was hardly that if
some of the stories told about him are true.

One of his cronies was a short deaf mute called
'Spoon' because of his special talent for scooping
corpses out of coffins. There is a story that Merry
Andrew and Spoon went to a house to pick up the body
of a woman they had agreed to purchase as soon as she
died, only to be informed by the old woman who had
looked after her that she had changed her mind. 'A light
has come down upon me frae heaven, an' I canna,' she
explained. 'Light frae heaven!' exclaimed Merry
Andrew. 'Will that show the doctors how to cut a cancer
out o' ye, ye auld fule?'

The 'Screw' and 'Praying Howard' were other
members of the Edinburgh fraternity, the latter so called
because he would attend funerals offering prayer and
comfort to the mourners, then give his colleagues the
tip-off as to the nature of the deceased, the site of the
grave, and so on. A former plasterer by the name of
Mowatt was called 'Mouldiewarp' (a northern colloquial
name for a mole) because he did most of the digging.

One much-repeated tale goes that Merry Andrew's
sister died, and was buried as Penicuik, whence he
intended to repair in order to present his sister's body,
for a small sum of course, as a contribution to science.
But Mouldiewarp and Spoon decided to beat him to it,
as they bore him a grudge for having cheated them out

of ten shillings. (Honour among thieves was scarcely an ethical principle of this profession.) As Mouldiewarp and Spoon were busy digging in the silent kirkyard in the middle of the night, they were suddenly confronted by a white apparition rising with arms spread out from behind a tombstone. Frozen rigid momentarily, the two fled in terror. The 'ghost' was Merry Andrew, who had cottoned on to their game, and chuckling to himself that 'The Spune maun dae wi'out its porritch this time,' he duly delivered the late Miss Merrilees to one of the tenants of Edinburgh's Surgeons' Square.[8]

Lingering belief in ghosts was of some assistance to body-snatchers, more especially in the north, perhaps, where superstition was slower in giving way to materialistic scorn than in the south. Spreading rumours of haunted churchyards could help to ensure that no one went anywhere near them at night. There is a frequently told tale about two Bristol medical students being frightened off by ghosts whilst raising a corpse from the churchyard at Long Ashton. One of the students, the son of a dissenting minister in Bristol, suffered such a severe shock that he died soon afterwards. It is assumed that the ghosts were professional body-snatchers who resented the intrusion of amateurs.[9]

Certain districts of some towns and cities came to be associated with body-snatchers. The St Pancras area of London was a well-known hive of activity at one time, as well as the area south of the river around Southwark and Bermondsey, where the Crouch gang hung out, within easy reach of the United Hospitals – Guy's and St Thomas's. In Glasgow the wynds off Trongate harboured many sack-'em-up men, the Old Wynd being especially infamous, and in Edinburgh the slums fringeing High Street and Canongate were well-known resorts of the resurrectionists.

Meanwhile, in England, the pace of progress in anatomy and surgery was being set by Sir Astley Paston Cooper. A Norfolk man, Cooper was still quite young when already a surgeon at Guy's, a lecturer at St Thomas's, and a Fellow of the Royal Society. In 1807 he published an important work, *On Hernia*, the operation for which was, until then, often unsuccessful because knowledge of the local anatomy was inadequate. He was made a baronet in consideration of having performed a successful operation to remove a tumour from George IV's head in 1820, and soon other members of the royal family, as well as the Prime Minister and the Duke of Wellington, numbered among his patients. In 1827 he was elected President of the Royal College of Surgeons.

Sir Astley frequently dissected animals when human subjects were not available, paying for dead dogs brought to him and arranging to receive animals that died in the Royal Menagerie at the Tower of London, including an elephant on one occasion. But of course he really wanted a continuous supply of human subjects and, seemingly omnipotent in his dealings with the body-snatchers, he came to be known as 'King of the Resurrectionists'. He had no illusions about the amoral and brutish character of the men he employed, but he knew that until the law was changed he had no option but to pay for their services if he was to continue his work. Sir Astley paid Bill Hollis and Tom Vaughan thirteen pounds twelve shillings in 1820 to fetch from the churchyard at Beccles the body of a man he had operated on nearly a quarter of a century earlier, and of whose death he had been notified by a local surgeon. He once paid seventy-two pounds to a London body-snatcher for six subjects, and if any of his regular suppliers fell foul of the law, he felt morally bound to intercede on their behalf, sometimes appealing directly to the Home Secretary.

An unsigned and undated note among Sir Astley's papers reads: 'Sir, I have been informed you are in the habit of purchasing bodys and allowing the person a sum weekly; knowing a poor woman that is desirous of doing so, I have taken the liberty of calling to know the truth.' On the back of this note Sir Astley wrote: 'Answer. The *truth* is that you deserve to be hanged for such an unfeeling offer. A.C.'

Sir Astley was not quite so sensitive as this suggests, however. He was an acquisitive dealer in death himself, and not especially particular about how bodies had been obtained as long as they were suitable for his purposes. On one occasion he paid a body-snatcher named Page over thirty-five pounds for three corpses, only to be ordered to return them when it was found that they had been taken from the mortuary at Newington. They had not been buried and Sir Astley had not enquired too closely about their origins.

Cooper boasted once to a committee of enquiry: 'There is no person, let his situation be what it may, whom, if I were disposed to dissect, I could not obtain.' His nephew and biographer Bransby Cooper wrote: 'I once heard Sir Astley, when wishing to expose to a certain person the power of these men, and his influence over them, offer to procure, within three days, the body of a dignified official personage, who had been buried in a place apparently of impenetrable security. I have every reason to believe, that had he chosen, he could have effected this object.'

As medical schools grew and training increased with advances in knowledge and the rapidly rising urban population, so the demand for corpses grew and the pace of body-snatching accelerated. The cathedral graveyard and the Ramshorn burial ground in Glasgow were being raided almost every night during one period. One professional claimed that he had once dug up twenty-three bodies in four nights.

Press and public agitation grew, fuelled by wild rumours and unjustified terrors in the absence of legislation and established fact. One of the rumours that gained wide currency was that some of the doctors kept vultures for disposing of cadavers once they had served their purposes.[10] A correspondent to the editor of a Liverpool literary and scientific journal suggested that: 'It is no uncommon occurrence, if the professor happen to leave the room, for the students to cut off a large piece of the flesh, and throw it to any dog that should happen to be passing at the time.'[11]

'The most horrid Robbery of all robberies!!' screamed the headline of a broadsheet on the streets of Bristol in 1813 – 'The Graves Opened and the dead stolen!!!' On 18 November 1812, George and Elizabeth Elson had witnessed the burial of their young son William in the family grave at Bedminster churchyard. In June the following year, Elizabeth Elson's sister Mary died, and it was arranged that she should be buried in the same grave beneath the child's coffin. But when the sexton opened the grave, the boy's body was not there. He did not reveal this fact until the day of the sister's funeral, but said that he had opened several other graves round about, 'to see if peradventure the child had gone into any other.'[12]

A few days before Christmas in 1813, the windows of Glasgow University's Professor of Anatomy, Dr James Jeffrey, were broken by an angry mob which had got wind of the disappearance of a Mrs McAlister's body from Ramshorn churchyard. A search warrant was issued and peace officers accompanied Mrs McAlister's dentist, and two people who had known the woman, to the College Street dissecting rooms of a newly appointed lecturer, Dr Granville Sharp Pattison. There they found parts of a female human body in a tub of water. A severed finger was recognized as Mrs McAlister's wedding-ring finger, and the dentist identified teeth in a jawbone as hers. Dr Pattison and a lecturer on surgery, Andrew Russell, were arrested, together with two students who were present, Robert Munro and John McLean. As they left the building, stones thrown by the crowd rained down on them. Officers continued to search the building, and found further human remains under the floorboards.

All four men were charged before the High Court of Justiciary in Edinburgh, in June 1814, with stealing the body of Mrs McAlister, conveying it to the dissecting room, and mangling the body to prevent its recognition. Counsel for Dr Pattison immediately requested that the case be heard in camera, owing to the somewhat delicate nature of the evidence he would present. This request was refused, although their lordships instructed the newspapermen to give as little publicity as possible to the case, as the details would 'only tend to inflame the minds of the vulgar.' The *Glasgow Herald*'s report stated simply that the medical witnesses had found it impossible to say whether the body was Mrs McAlister's or not. In fact, the defence had lost little time in playing its trump card. Mrs McAlister, they pointed out, was a mother, but a significant part of the body alleged to be hers had belonged to a virgin. Russell and McLean were declared Not Guilty, by direction of the Lord Justice Clerk, and the case against Pattison and Munro was found Not Proven.[13]

Dr Pattison found it necessary to emigrate to the United States soon after this affair, having been cited also as the co-respondent in a divorce case. Scotland's loss was undoubtedly America's gain, despite his reputation with the public on both sides of the Atlantic. He had risen in seven years from being an anatomy assistant to election as a member of the Faculty of

Physicians and Surgeons and being appointed surgeon
to Glasgow Royal Infirmary. He held various important
posts in the United States, founded the Bellevue
Medical Centre in New York, and sold his private
anatomical museum to the University of Maryland.

Five years after this local sensation in Glasgow, Dr
Jeffrey himself added to the public's fear of the doctors
when the story got around of his part in his lecturer
Andrew Ure's experiments with galvanism – the study
of the effects of electrical currents passed through the
body. A collier named Matthew Clydesdale was hanged
for murder, and his body handed over to the university
medical school, in accordance with the law. There is
some contradiction in reports of what happened, but all
agree on the essential facts. Students and the public
gathered to witness the proposed experiment; the
corpse was placed in a sitting position in a chair; the
handles from the galvanic battery were put into the
hands and the current was switched on. The startled –
not to say horrified – spectators saw the chest heave
and the 'dead' man stood up. Whilst many rushed out
of the room in terror at this sight, Dr Jeffrey, it was said,
quickly and coolly cut the man's throat with his scalpel,
and so was technically guilty of murder, though
theoretically the man had already been executed. The
panic caused by this incident led to the banning of
anatomical experiments in public and of all experiments
with electricity on corpses.

In October 1819, the Chatham coach delivered to the
Cross Keys in London's Cheapside two pieces of
luggage – a hamper and a heavy item tied up in a mat.
The former was addressed to Mr Joseph Wright of
33 Old Street, and the latter to a Mr William Simpson at
126 Oxford Street. Both were to be left at the inn until
called for, but Mr Simpson's consignment was soon
giving off an unpleasant smell, and the innkeeper

decided to open it. He found the corpse of an old woman. The local beadle was called, and he opened the hamper, which contained a man's corpse. The coroner was informed, and the authorities then waited for someone to collect the luggage. It turned out to be a man who called himself Williams, and having paid the innkeeper the bill for carriage, he was arrested as he prepared to take the parcels away. He was, in fact, George Martin, one of Crouch's cronies, who was acting on this occasion on behalf of William Millard, the dissecting room superintendent of St Thomas's Hospital.

The *Edinburgh Weekly Chronicle* assumed a level-headed approach at the beginning of a leader it devoted about this time to the existing system of supplying teachers of anatomy with subjects, referring to its advantages and 'the indispensability of it in the present state of the law'. But the paper then completely lost its head in criticizing official interference with bodies shipped from Ireland, arguing that 'for every Irish subject they seize they insure the rifling of some Scotch grave'.

The government, meanwhile, did nothing. It had other things on its mind – the war in Europe; the price of bread; the Luddite riots. The latter had led Spencer Perceval's government, amid much agitated talk of sedition, political insurrection and the consequences of revolution in France, to make machine-breaking a capital offence in 1812, while digging up a grave and removing the corpse for violation by surgeons was no more than a misdemeanour. Magistrates, however, would sometimes convict body-snatchers for trespassing or causing a disturbance, when stealing a body was no crime. But in the same week that two men were fined twenty pounds each at Liverpool for raising the bodies of a man and two women from St John's churchyard, three children were fined at Ormskirk for whistling in the street.[14]

The prosecution and punishment of resurrection men

by the authorities in Scotland drove the trade across the border to some extent, and grave-robbers in London and other parts of England did good business supplying bodies to Edinburgh and Glasgow, where it was becoming increasingly difficult to beat the various methods employed to protect the dead.

From various items of information given here and there by doctors and others at the time, it is possible to estimate, very conservatively, that more than a thousand corpses a year were being lifted from burial grounds in England and Scotland in the first decade of the nineteenth century. That is to say, on average, at least three bodies were being dug up every night somewhere in Britain. But they were not enough to satisfy the doctors' needs.

The entrance on the scene of a capable and willing army of professional grave-robbers did not mean that anatomy teachers and their students gave up their own body-snatching activities entirely. The need for subjects was ever greater, and the specialists could not always be relied on. It was hardly to be expected that such men would be scrupulously honest in their business dealings. One Edinburgh resurrectionist obtained an advance of two pounds ten shillings from an anatomy lecturer on a body he had promised, in order to pay some initial expenses (bribes, no doubt) and then sent a box filled with rubbish. Four men were subsequently apprehended in connection with this incident, and in due course sentenced to two months imprisonment – for fraud!

One body was sold by resurrection men to an Edinburgh surgeon named Lizars, then stolen back from his dissecting room by the same men and sold again to Robert Knox, the crooks getting twenty-five pounds for the one corpse.

When Joshua Brookes, who ran a private anatomy

school in London's Blenheim Street, refused to give body-snatchers five pounds in advance for a promised corpse, the disgruntled resurrectionists dumped badly decomposed bodies at each end of the street late one night. The ghastly discovery was made by two young women early the next morning, and police had to protect Brookes from a furious crowd which soon gathered outside his premises.

Patrick Murphy, who succeeded Crouch as leader of the Southwark gang, had a grudge against Brookes, and he sent one of his men who was unknown to Brookes to claim that a body which Brookes had bought from Murphy was his sister. He demanded to be allowed to take it away for decent reburial. The doctors could never refuse such requests, and the man left with the corpse, only – as Brookes later learned – to sell it at once to another surgeon. Murphy once made a hundred and forty-four pounds for twelve corpses in a single day, selling them all to two clients, one of whom was Astley Cooper.

In 1807, a teenage medical student named Taylor agreed to pay a man named Smith for the body of an illegitimate baby, two or three months old – the child of a girl named Kelly. When he went to collect it, he found the unwanted infant still very much alive. Smith thereupon killed the child on the spot, clutching it by the throat and holding its head under water. Taylor took it away, but the surgeon to whom he was apprenticed refused to accept it, and Taylor hid the body. It was found two weeks later, and both men were duly apprehended and tried for murder. Although Smith was convicted, Taylor was acquitted, the jury being apparently impressed by the argument that his mere presence was not enough to justify conviction, and notwithstanding Smith's statement that Taylor had told him how to kill the child. No doubt the student's tender age worked in his favour.

In Dublin, John Green Crosse, the Norwich surgeon who taught anatomy at Trinity College in 1813-14, bought bodies from professional resurrectionists and also went out on expeditions himself, aware that if he failed to satisfy his students with practical demonstrations, they would go elsewhere, and the medical school would lose its reputation. Bully's Acre, the burial ground beside the Royal Hospital on the west side of the city, where many paupers and vagrants were buried, was a reliable source of subjects, and Crosse went there several times in the early months of 1814, as his diary shows:

> *January 2nd*
> Was with resurrection men at Bullies Acre from one till three ...
> *January 25th*
> Last Friday was resurrecting unsuccessfully – not home till 6 in ye morning ...
> *March 7th*
> Have been resurrecting three times since the last adventure which I mentioned and with better success.'[15]

The regular night-shift at Bully's Acre would borrow picks and shovels kept at a nearby public house for the convenience of paupers' friends or relatives who wished to bury their dead themselves to save costs.

As the study of anatomy and surgery grew in Ireland, attracting large numbers of students each year, Irish anatomists began to complain at the export of so many subjects to England and Scotland, saying that there was now a shortage of bodies for their own use.

In Bristol in November 1822, three parish constables arrested six young men in the act of digging up a young woman's body at midnight in the churchyard at Bedminster. Pistols were fired and swords drawn in the ensuing struggle, before five of the men were taken into custody, the sixth managing to escape. The men, who turned out to be medical students, were tried at Wells for conspiracy, riot and assault, as well as for disturbing the grave. Their defence counsel admitted their guilt on all the charges except conspiracy, which he begged to have dropped from the indictment as it might interfere with their future careers as surgeons. It was a telling point. At length they were all let off with fines of five pounds each.[16]

Chapter IV: Doctors' Dilemmas

' ... the body-snatcher, far from being repelled by natural respect, was attracted by the ease and safety of the task. To bodies that had been lain in earth, in joyful expectation of a far different awakening, there came that hasty, lamp-lit, terror-haunted resurrection of the spade and mattock. The coffin was forced, the cerements torn, and the melancholy relics, clad in sack-cloth, after being rattled for hours on moonless by-ways, were at length exposed to uttermost indignities before a class of gaping boys.'

Robert Louis Stevenson
The Body-Snatcher, 1884

The doctors may have felt very uncomfortable about being forced into a business relationship with men from the lowest ranks of society, who were regarded by the public at large as positively evil and engaged in what has been called 'the foulest trade in human history'. There is a story that the wife of a Liverpool surgeon answered a knock at her door to find two rough-looking men outside, one of whom asked her, 'Do you think the Doctor wants a kid?'[1] But the medical men had little scruple about the principle of what they did, and were often arrogant about it. One professor at Aberdeen's Marischal College was reputed to arrive regularly in the quadrangle with a fresh corpse sitting beside him on the seat of his coach.

The law of supply and demand, in this trade as in any

other, meant that the purchasers who needed the goods
had to enter into fair agreements with the vendors, and
could not have things all their own way. True, when
Ben Crouch called his men out on strike in London, at
the commencement of the 1811 lecturing season, to
back his demand for an increase in prices, the
anatomists decided they could ride out this storm,
especially as there were plenty of dabblers in the trade
willing to undermine union solidarity by undercutting
the big boys. There was therefore no immediate
shortage of subjects, and Crouch had to order his men
back to work after a few weeks with a compromise
agreement that was very much in the surgeons' favour.
(Crouch and his men took their revenge on the
customers of the scabs, by breaking into the dissecting
rooms where the corpses lay and 'cutting' them; that is,
hacking and slashing them so severely that they were
no longer of any use to the anatomists.) But, generally
speaking, the doctors wanted all the 'things' they could
get hold of, and their deals with the resurrection men
perforce left aside all questions of medical ethics,
though in public they maintained the high-minded air
of altruistic men devoted exclusively to the public
well-being.

They were genuinely on the horns of a dilemma.
They had unquestionably made the government aware
of the problems they had in training the surgeons
required by a rapidly expanding population, and the
government had done nothing about it. The doctors
had to choose between continuing to support the illicit
trade in dead bodies, and cutting down their teaching
courses to the bare minimum that could be maintained
with the supply of executed criminals. They chose the
former, and in the opinion of many, chose wrongly.

They got away with their duplicity remarkably well
for a long time. Communications then were not what

they are today. Individual outrages were regularly reported in the local press, of course, but it dawned only slowly on the British public as a whole that isolated incidents heard of in one place one week and another the next were but the tip of an iceberg. Few people suspected in the first quarter of the nineteenth century that doctors and body-snatchers were in league on a scale that was a disgrace to the nation.

No doubt many of the doctors, as men of science, regarded the dead body merely as a clapped-out machine, and any religious attachment to it, as a sentimental delusion on the part of friends and relatives. This may have eased their consciences and reinforced their own convictions that they were acting in the best interests of the living. As long as the anatomists and the resurrection men were able to continue their trading in relative secrecy, they had nothing to fear. As with adultery, the biggest sin was in being found out. But unfortunately for the doctors, all events seemed to conspire against them.

The zealousness with which the Scots pursued and punished body-snatchers had, for some years, been leading to a situation in which the *Westminster Review* reported that: 'The Medical School at Edinburgh, in fact, is now subsisting entirely on its past reputation, and in the course of a few years it will be entirely at an end, unless the system be changed.' The difficulty of procuring subjects, the article continued, had led to many students, who were unable to pursue their studies properly, leaving the place in disgust.

In London, Thomas Wakley, a former pupil of Astley Cooper's and later the founder and editor of the medical journal the *Lancet*, was violently attacked at his home in Argyll Street in 1820 following rumours that he was the masked man who had carried out the sentence of the court by decapitating Arthur Thistlewood and his four fellow Cato Street conspirators after they had been hanged on the gallows at Newgate. The speed with which the job was done led spectators to conclude that the man was a skilled surgeon. In fact, it seems to have been a resurrection man named Parker who was paid by the sheriff to do the job – the last time this form of 'punishment' was carried out. Parker's eloquent self-testimonial to qualify him to assist the hangman James Botting was that he was practised at 'cutting off nobs for the purpose of getting the gnashers'. All the same, Wakley's house was burnt down, presumably by sympathizers of the hanged men who had plotted to overthrow the government.

Teachers of anatomy in provincial towns were experiencing the same difficulties as those in London and Edinburgh. Disturbances at Cambridge between students and populace had been fairly common since around 1730, when medical students had begun to dig up bodies in the churchyards of Cambridge and the surrounding villages.[2]

Provincial practitioners of body-snatching showed that they were certainly the equals of their counterparts in London and Edinburgh when it came to provoking public outrage. At Bristol in 1819, the body of a woman buried in St Augustine's churchyard was stolen from its grave the day after the funeral, and that evening, two men were seen carrying a sack into a greengrocer's shop in Lower College Street. Above the shop was a dissecting room shared by two or three local surgeons. A crowd soon gathered outside, and the husband of the dead woman forced an entry to the dissecting room, where he found the body of his late wife in a sack, and recovered it after a scuffle with a doctor who had to beat a hasty retreat to escape the furious mob. The parish offered a reward of fifty guineas for information leading to the conviction of the body-snatchers, but there is no record that they were ever caught.

Thomas Earl, one of the local anatomists, was widely rumoured to be the man who had brought the body to the dissecting room, but he indignantly denied it and offered a reward of five guineas to anyone who would reveal the author of 'so malicious and unjust an accusation'. The *Bristol Mirror*, meanwhile, carried an extraordinary article by an unnamed correspondent regretting that so much publicity was being given to the activities of the resurrectionists. It was, the writer believed, better that such matters be hidden from the public view altogether, because of the 'general unpleasant feeling which such facts must necessarily excite.'[3] In a letter to the editor of the *Bristol Observer*, a correspondent signing himself 'Quere' deplored the 'folly, the wickedness, and the barbarity of cutting up dead bodies for the benefit of the living', and wanted to know by what law those who disinterred corpses could be punished.

In Sunderland in 1823, a child's coffin was officially raised in order to bury it again in a different part of the churchyard, following the request of the child's father, a Captain Hedley. But the coffin was found to be empty, and investigation revealed two other empty coffins nearby. Two strangers who had been seen in the vicinity were apprehended, and in the lodgings of one of them, Captain Hedley's daughter was found, parcelled up and addressed to Leith Street, Edinburgh. The two men, Thompson and Weatherley, both from Scotland, got three months in prison and fines of six pence each. There was evidence that they had been active in the area for some time.

Not that Sunderland did not have its own native body-snatchers. A local publican, one of the parish church's bell-ringers, was suspected of having an interest in the trade; and there is a story that one resurrection man accidentally hanged himself when trying to get a sacked and roped body over the churchyard wall. The body fell on one side of the wall hoisting up the man, with the rope round his neck, on the other.[4]

At Norwich, early in 1823, suspicions were aroused at the coach office of the Rampant Horse Inn by the frequency of consignments in trunks addressed to 'J.C. Roberts, Esq., London, to be left at the Flower Pot in Bishopsgate Street till called for.' The clerk was told to detain whoever brought the next such trunk. On 15 February a man turned up with a trunk which was opened to reveal the body of an old man, later identified as Thomas Brundall, who had been buried in Lakenham churchyard two days earlier. The transporter of the trunk was one Ephraim Ulph, who said he had been paid by a man named Collins to deliver it. Collins lodged with a Mrs Rice, and employed Ulph to look after his horse and gig. Joseph Collins and an accomplice, Thomas Crowe, were arrested and brought to trial in due course at Norwich Quarter Sessions. The city gaoler, who had arrested them, said that he had found in the possession of the two accused a number of skeleton keys, which turned out to fit the locks of several local churches, including Lakenham. He had also found various tools of the body-snatchers' trade, and two teeth, which appeared to fit gaps in the dead man's upper jaw. Collins and Crowe were each sentenced to three months imprisonment and a fine of fifty pounds, the City Steward remarking that if experience and skill in anatomy were to be obtained 'only by such means as the prisoners had made use of it would be better for ancient ignorance to return'.[5]

In June 1823 a man living in Pomona Street, Liverpool, went into his cellar, which he had let some time before to a respectable young man for the storage of dried goods, and found a parcel containing a human head in a state of putrefaction. The ghastly news spread quickly and an agitated crowd soon gathered outside the premises, but no prosecution seems to have resulted from this discovery. In the following week's newspaper, however, this letter to the editors was published: 'Gentlemen, There is a very unpleasant and extraordinary sensation which affects the *olfactory nerves* of all sensitive passengers as they pass by the gas lamp-post in Great George-street, at the top of St. Vincent-street. I have been annoyed by it for more than a week. It appears to arise out of a cellar close by; it cannot be a stream of gas. I am afraid of ghosts! or I would step into the cellar to see if there are any *dry goods* (alias, human heads) similar to those found in a cellar in Pomona-street. Yours, GO LOOK!'[6] Was it a hoax in poor taste? I cannot find evidence that any horrible discovery resulted from the accusation.

In Manchester, however, suspicions led to more positive results. Neighbours' apprehensions were aroused early in 1824 by the nocturnal comings and goings of several men who rented a stable at the end of Back King Street. The men were also seen unloading packing cases from a gig. The neighbours reported these incidents to the police office, and a Mr Lavender and two beadles went to the stable, where they found two men with three packing cases addressed to London. One of the cases was opened and found to contain two bodies. The two men, William Johnson and William Harrison, admitted that the other two cases had similar contents, and they were arrested and taken before a magistrate. There was no case without proof that they had stolen the bodies, however, and the six corpses were exhibited for identification at the George Inn. Five of them were duly recognized as persons buried in a common grave at a Catholic burial ground in

Granby Row between 25 January and 13 February. The six bodies – two children, two women and two elderly men – had been doubled up in cases which were each two feet long and thirteen inches wide, and two feet deep.[7]

In January 1825, two men were detained by police officers in Portsmouth, as they were boarding a London-bound coach with a trunk. This contained a corpse which had been dug up from a burial ground at Gosport. The grave-digger there confessed that he had dug up the body for the two men, and that he had supplied four other bodies in return for thirty shillings and a 'plentiful supply of gin and beer'.[8]

Men who were brought to court for body-snatching put up some remarkable defences. In Hertfordshire, a man at Whitewell accused of digging up and selling the body of his own grandmother defended himself with irrefutable logic by arguing that it was surely more fitting that he, rather than some complete stranger, should have the money![9] But a more successful plea was put up in 1825 when two resurrection men, James May and John Jerome, were brought before the Middlesex Sessions after being chased by a watchman in the churchyard of St Leonard, Shoreditch, and arrested in possession of a spade, a pick-axe and a body in a sack. They got off by claiming that they were not the body-snatchers, who had escaped in the darkness, but public-spirited passers-by who had come to the aid of the watchman. This defence, not unnaturally, became rather celebrated among denizens of the criminal underworld, May, in particular, being a well-known professional body-snatcher.

In the same year William Clarke, alias Taylor, got twelve months' imprisonment after admitting in court that he had raised forty-five bodies in five months from their graves in the churchyard at Walcot, a suburb of

Bath, and sent them to London by coach. Two of them, he said in mitigation, had been specifically for Sir Astley Cooper to practise on before he operated on the King!

The magistrate sitting when two resurrectionists were brought before the bench in June 1830 was treated to a speech from one defendant complaining that the police would be 'much better engaged in looking after thieves and house-breakers than apprehending respectable men who lived by supplying the faculty with subjects for dissection.'

In 1823, William Millard, who had been a dissecting room assistant at St Thomas's Hospital, and had turned to body-snatching after his dismissal for dishonest practices, died of gaol fever in Cold Baths Fields prison, just before Sir Astley Cooper succeeded in persuading the Home Secretary to release him. Sir Astley did this in spite of the fact that Millard had been supplying a rival, Edward Grainger, a former pupil of Cooper's who had set up an anatomy school where he lectured in both winter and summer. (Grainger's first premises were in a disused Roman Catholic chapel in Webb Street, where he eventually built his own theatre, close to Guy's and St Thomas's, and very convenient for the Crouch gang.)

Cooper wished to lecture in the summer months as well as in winter, aware that too long a break between terms meant that students forgot much of what they had been taught. But apart from any other difficulties, this would mean an even greater demand for subjects, and Sir Astley sent letters to leading surgeons and teachers of anatomy in which he asked for any ideas they might have on how more bodies might be obtained for the capital's anatomy schools. Sir Astley's letter to a surgeon named Lane, for instance, read:

'My dear Sir,
    Will you write me word what you consider to be

the *Cause* and the *Remedy* for the Deficient Supply for Anatomical purposes.

> I am
> Yours truly
> Astley Cooper

A Committee is applying help to the subject.[10]

When Cooper had the doctors' replies, he sent them to Home Secretary Peel. The consensus of opinion was that unclaimed bodies of those who died in prisons and hospitals should be granted to, and distributed by, the Royal College of Surgeons. It was revealed that both the London Hospital and Guy's already had a policy, hitherto strictly secret, of allowing bodies that were not claimed by relatives to be dissected in their lecture rooms.

Other hospitals likewise preferred the public to believe the fiction that the bodies of those who died were sacred, but in fact they sometimes knowingly buried bodies only to buy them back later from the body-snatchers. In 1831 the Leeds Workhouse Board began allowing the bodies of those who died without relatives to be handed over to the surgeons.

In Liverpool, undeterred by the fact that the city had no properly constituted medical school at the time, the Literary and Philosophical Society resolved in 1825 to send a petition to Parliament through the local MP, William Huskisson, calling for a change in the law. They also submitted a petition to the King for consideration of the case of two resurrection men, Stewart and Armstrong, who had been given fines and prison sentences for lifting bodies from local churchyards. The petition to the House of Commons, though based on 'powerful arguments' in Huskisson's view, came to nothing, but as it summarizes clearly the situation as it appeared to men of science at the time, its text is given as Appendix A. As for the petition to the King, the Home Secretary's reply to Huskisson was as follows:

Whitehall, 25th June, 1825

Sir,
   Having referred to the Recorder of Liverpool the Petition which you transmitted to me on behalf of Thos. Stewart and Robt. Armstrong, two prisoners in the gaol of Liverpool under a Sentence of Imprisonment and Fine for stealing dead bodies, I am sorry to acquaint you that his report on the case is of such a nature that I cannot consistently with my public duty recommend the Prisoners to his Majesty for any mitigation of their sentence.
   I have the honour to be, Sir, your most obedient and humble Servant,

Robt. Peel[11]

Peel was, however, sympathetic to the doctors' dilemma. He had promised Cooper further discussions on this delicate matter, and quietly helped by ensuring that bodies imported in crates from Ireland were generally allowed to pass through Customs on his authority. Bodies were also being imported from France, coming chiefly via Le Havre, with Peel's nervous acquiescence. This was all right as far as it went, but it did not go far enough for the doctors, whilst to the general public, becoming more aware as time passed of the real scale of grave-robbery and dissection, it went much *too* far. The public became increasingly incensed as the grave-robbers continued to defy all concepts of human decency and the best efforts – under the existing law – to suppress them.
   In the first days of 1826 at Newcastle, a box being carried by coach from Leeds to a 'Mr Simpson' at Edinburgh fell open to reveal the naked corpse of a

man, who proved to be Thomas Daniel. He had been buried on New Year's Day in St John's churchyard in Leeds. A young man named George Cox, who had delivered the box to the Leeds coach depot, was arrested and charged with stealing the body, and despite his plea that he had been employed by a Jew to make the box and deliver it, not knowing what it contained, he was found guilty and sentenced to six months' imprisonment.

A box opened at the King's Arms in Lancaster, in October of the same year, was found to contain the putrid bodies of a middle-aged woman and an infant boy. The box measured 22 × 15 × 12 inches, and was addressed to 'Archibald Young, Esq., 59 South Bridge-street, Edinburgh'. It had arrived at Lancaster on the coach from Liverpool, and passengers had complained of the smell, saying they would not proceed on their journey with that coach if the box was not removed when they reached Lancaster. The clerk at the coach depot then sent the box to the fly-boat warehouse to be sent on by canal, but the men there refused to have the offensive box on their premises. The origin of the box could only be traced back as far as Manchester, but it had already been giving off a bad smell there, and had no doubt come from Ireland. The coroner's verdict on the two bodies was 'Found in a box, Lancaster.'[12]

Complaints in the same month by dockers at St George's Dock, Liverpool, about the awful stench from three casks marked 'Bitter Salts', which they put aboard a smack bound for Leith, led to the discovery of eleven corpses, pickled in brine and packed in salt. There were six male and five female bodies. They were all naked, and had apparently died natural deaths. A police surgeon who examined them thought they had been dead six or seven days. The shipping note accompanying the casks read: 'Please ship on board the *Latona* three casks of Bitter Salts, from Mr Brown, Agent, Liverpool, to Mr G.H. Ironson, Edinburgh.' George Leech, the carter who had delivered the casks to George's Dock Passage, was soon traced, and he stated that he had been hired by a Scotsman to convey the casks to the dock from a cellar at 12 Hope Street. Several officers went to this address and found it to be the house of a clergyman, Revd James McGowan, who ran a school there. He had let the cellar, since the previous January, to a man named Henderson, who had said he was a cooper. Some of Revd McGowan's pupils had complained of an offensive smell coming from the cellar, but had merely been told to open a window. When the police gained entry to the cellar, they found twenty-two more corpses, comprising nine men, five women, five boys and three girls. They also found a brass syringe, probably used to inject hot wax into the veins of corpses as a preservative. The police surgeon, Thomas Davis, supposed all the bodies to have been disinterred, from the evidence of a piece of thread on one of the women's toes, commonly used to hold the feet of corpses together. As some of the bodies were in an advanced state of decomposition, the coroner ordered their immediate reburial. There was evidence that some of them, at least, had been raised from the parish churchyard.

The Hope Street gang responsible for this outrage proved elusive, but the first man to be brought to justice was a young Scot named James Donaldson, who was recognized by several witnesses as one of those who came to the cellar frequently with casks on a hand-cart. During the course of his trial, a witness said that a tierce full of brine in the cellar had been found to contain the bodies of babies, and this evidence made the foreman of the jury feel so ill that he had to leave the court to recover. Donaldson was found guilty and given twelve months in the Kirkdale House of Correction, as well as being fined fifty pounds.

A few days later two more resurrectionists were arrested in connection with more corpses, discovered before they left Liverpool for Edinburgh. One of these men had on him a letter about dead bodies addressed to 'John Mack, Gamekeeper' from Edinburgh. At the Epiphany Sessions in January these two – Patrick McGregor and John Ross – were identified as members of the Hope Street gang and given twelve months' imprisonment and fined twenty-five pounds each. They claimed that they had been hired by medical students of various universities and had been driven to the work by their poverty, and this may well have been true. One of them was identified by the carter, Leech, as the man who had hired him, but none of the three convicted men, it seems, was the 'Mr Henderson' who had rented the cellar from Revd McGowan in the first place. He was never traced.[13]

Nottingham was infected by the evil in 1827, when two men already familiar to us, Hollis and Vaughan, were arrested with a third, going under the name of Giles, after staff at Pickford's office grew suspicious at the number of boxes and hampers suddenly being sent to London. One such box eventually being examined, it was found to contain the corpses of a woman and a child. Following identification of the bodies, the local vicar allowed relatives anxious about their loved-ones to open their graves in the parish churchyard and it was discovered that thirty-four bodies were missing. Parents were seen carrying away the empty coffins and grave-clothes of their children, and one man set off for London to try to recover his son's body. What arrangements had been made for these bodies in London, the *Nottingham Journal* observed, 'those in Lincoln-Inn-Fields (sic) can perhaps tell; but we caution them against making another attempt of this nature in this town.'[14] Lincoln's Inn Fields, of course, was the address of the Royal College of Surgeons.

In May 1827, a Manchester grave-digger, John Eaton, was indicted at the New Bailey Quarter Sessions for felony. He was the sexton of St George's Chapel near Oldham Road, and was charged with stealing a coffin belonging to one Abel Buckley. The prisoner lived in a house adjoining the chapel, and when Thomas Holme, a special constable and churchwarden, overheard a conversation between a hackney coachman and a man named Thomas which aroused his suspicions, he went with another man to Eaton's door and gained entry to a vault under the chapel, where Eaton kept fowls and pigs. He found there, in addition to the livestock, fifteen coffins, six of which were empty, the others containing decomposing corpses. In Eaton's house Mr Holme found three more coffins with putrid corpses in them, and in the privy, another body in a coffin. One of the empty coffins in the cellar had a plate on it inscribed, 'John Buckley, aged 3 years, 1827'. Challenged by Holme about the coffins in general and the one with the plate on it in particular, Eaton said, 'It's nothing to do with you, I put in what I have a mind,' and declared that he had found the Buckley coffin empty in the graveyard a day or two after the funeral. Eaton's wife said the coffin in the privy had been put there unknown to them.

Eaton's defence counsel at his trial challenged Holme's right to have entered the premises without a warrant, and asked James Thomas, who had accompanied Holme in his search of the premises, if he was not aware that it was usual to bury several bodies in one large grave, and for the sexton to keep them until he had a sufficient number. Thomas did *not* know that.

'If he kept them till he could fill a grave you would not think that wrong?'

'I did not think it right,' Thomas replied.

Sarah Buckley, mother of the child whose coffin plate had been found, testified that she and her husband had attended the funeral of their son at St George's Chapel, and had seen the prisoner begin to fill in the grave with earth after the coffin had been lowered into it. Counsel for the defence then suggested that the prisoner had clearly not stolen the coffin, and if he had only taken the body, that was not a felony. The chairman of the justices pointed out that it was possible he had stolen the graveclothes, although no evidence was offered on that score. Another witness testified that part of the cellar was used as a vault for stillborn infants, and at least two and possibly three of the corpses found were those of stillborn babies.

Eaton himself was not called to the witness stand, although he had stated to a magistrate at the preliminary hearing that he knew that bodies were continually being stolen from the graveyard, and had told the owners so. The judge disposed of a few red herrings, such as the question of whether the burial ground was consecrated or not, and directed the jury to consider only whether or not the sexton had stolen the Buckley coffin. They decided he had, and he was sentenced to six months' hard labour.[15]

And so the sordid business went on, increasing month by month, becoming ever more obtrusive, and causing swelling public horror at the desecration of graves. Then early in 1828 matters came to a head for the doctors.

William Gill, a surgeon who taught anatomy at his private school in Seel Street, Liverpool, was fined for *receiving* the corpse of a young woman named Harrison, knowing it to have been disinterred, for the purpose of dissection. The corpse was found, with the skin stripped from the face, in the house next door, which

Gill owned. The body had been taken from its grave in the parish churchyard at Walton, and Gill was also charged, along with the already infamous local body-snatcher Thomas Stewart, with digging up the body, but he was found not guilty on that count.

Dr Gill did not deny the charge of having the body in his possession, but read a prepared statement in his own defence, pointing out the inconsistency of the law in punishing those who practised surgery without proper qualifications and at the same time denying them the means of qualifying. He added that the remedy was to allow those who died in workhouses and hospitals without friends or relatives to be used for dissection, and that the problem could be solved secretly, if necessary, without the violation of decency. 'It is thus the continental schools are supplied; no graves are ever disturbed on the Continent.' The chairman of the bench pointed out, however, that the question was not whether the law was defective, but whether it had been infringed. It had, and Dr Gill was fined thirty pounds.[16]

This conviction for *possession* was an alarming interpretation of the law for the doctors, quite different from the customary procedure under which, at Bristol earlier in the same year, a magistrate had fined two surgeons, Drs Riley and Wallis, six pounds when they had actually been caught in Brislington churchyard with a shovel, an outsize corkscrew, rope and a sack.[17]

Surgeons and anatomists now protested that they were completely unaware that their practice of paying for corpses for dissection was against the law, and set about bombarding Parliament with strong representations and appeals for some change in the law that would permit them to continue their teaching and studies in the interests of mankind within the law, if what they were doing was outside it. Members of

Parliament voiced the concerns of the Edinburgh College of Surgeons, the Hunterian Society, Guy's Hospital, and many individual surgeons and schools of anatomy. Two hundred doctors and students in Bristol sent a petition pointing out that the knowledge of anatomy which was properly required by the medical examining boards could only be obtained by violation of the law.

The government responded by appointing a Select Committee to enquire into 'the manner of obtaining Subjects for Dissection in the Schools of Anatomy, and into the State of the Law affecting the Persons employed in obtaining and dissecting Bodies.' The committee's chairman was Henry Warburton, MP for Bridport. Robert Peel was one of its members. It would seem from Sir Astley Cooper's notes to his colleagues asking for their ideas that he had known about the setting-up of a committee for some time, and it was probably he who instigated it in collaboration with Warburton, the Commons spokesman for the medical profession.

Henry Warburton was the son of a timber merchant, and entered the timber trade himself after his education at Eton and Cambridge, but subsequently abandoned commercial life to follow his interests in science and politics. He became a Fellow of the Royal Society, and was returned to Parliament for Bridport in 1826, being re-elected in six subsequent elections until he resigned his seat when there was a whiff of bribery and corruption in the air. He then became MP for Kendal for four years before his retirement from politics. He was known as an exceptionally hard-working Member, often in the House for twelve hours without a break. He was a keen supporter of the foundation of London University. From the time he was appointed chairman of the Select Committee, he devoted himself with energy and stamina to the cause of reform in the teaching of anatomy.

The Committee recognized that the present difficulties arose from that 'natural feeling which leads men to treat with reverence the remains of the Dead: and the same feeling has prompted them, in almost all times and countries, to regard with repugnance, and to persecute, Anatomy.' It pointed out, however, that of 3,744 people who died in the London workhouses in 1827, 3,103 were buried at the expense of the parishes, and about 1,108 of those were with no friends or relations present. If these bodies had been granted to the anatomists, the supply of fresh corpses would have exceeded those provided by the resurrection men. The Committee observed that, under the present law, 'there is scarcely a student or teacher of Anatomy in England who ... is not indictable for a misdemeanour'.

The Committee questioned many London-based witnesses, ranging from Sir Astley Cooper and other leading medical men, right down to professional body-snatchers, and also took written evidence from provincial witnesses. The doctors included such notable figures as Sir Benjamin Brodie of St George's Hospital, soon to become physician to William IV and then to Queen Victoria; Sir Henry Halford, who had attended George II and IV and was now President of the Royal College of Physicians; Alexander Cromar, President of the Aberdeen Medico-Chirurgical Society; Doctors Abernethy and Lawrence of St Bartholomew's; J.H. Green, Surgeon to St Thomas's; Joshua Brookes, Caesar Hawkins, Herbert Mayo and R.D. Grainger, all lecturers in anatomy; Dr Granville Sharp Pattison, formerly of Glasgow University and lately practising in America; and many others.

The doctors were unanimous in maintaining that the four or five hundred bodies dissected per year in the

London schools were not enough. Brodie thought that at least seven hundred were needed to teach the subject adequately, and Cooper said there would be many more than the current seven hundred students in London, if only those obliged to study abroad would remain in England. He said there were ten teachers of anatomy then in London. These were Guy's, St Thomas's, St Bartholomew's and the London Hospital, the Windmill Street school, and Messrs Grainger, Tyrrell, Carpue, Bennett, Dermott and Sleigh.[18]

Sir Astley also told the Committee that Sir Robert Peel had done his best to discourage prosecution of doctors and body-snatchers, and to 'relieve us from the difficulties under which we labour, and which impede the progress of science, and will soon render the profession a curse, instead of a blessing.' The need to learn anatomy, which could only be done properly from human subjects, was essential. 'You must employ medical men,' Cooper went on, 'whether they be ignorant or informed; but if you have none but ignorant medical men, it is you who suffer from it; and the fact is, that the want of subjects will soon lead to your becoming the unhappy victims of operations founded and performed in ignorance.'

At almost exactly the time when Sir Astley was testifying to the Select Committee, he paid half the expenses of bailing Tom Vaughan (who seems to have been a singularly careless or unlucky member of his profession, having been in trouble at Yarmouth, Norwich and Colchester, among other places). Sir Astley's account book for May 1828 includes the items:

6th. Paid Vaughan's wife 6s.
29th. Paid Vaughan for 26 weeks confinement, at 10s per week, £13.

Sir Astley made the curious observation to the Committee members, however, regarding the body-snatchers, that 'As to myself, if they would imagine that I would make a good subject, they would not have the smallest scruple, if they could do the thing undiscovered, to make a subject of me.' Did he mean by this that they would murder him, or simply that they would dig him up after his death? If he was referring to murder, did he have knowledge of such crimes having been committed? If he meant the latter, was it supposed to shock anyone? Why should *his* corpse be any more inviolate than anyone else's when little regard for the sanctity of the dead was shown either by doctors or resurrection men? Was Cooper, in fact, *afraid* of being dissected himself?

Sir Benjamin Brodie certainly had murder in mind when he told the Committee he considered it 'a dangerous thing to society' that body-snatchers should be able to get ten guineas for a body. There was not a great deal of unanimity among the doctors on some of the other points of detail. Sir Astley Cooper said that suicides would make bad subjects, 'because all persons who die suddenly, become soon putrid'. But Brodie said that 'a man who destroys himself by cutting his carotid arteries makes a very good subject for dissection.'

The Committee members were keen to know the current price one could obtain for a corpse. Cooper said that in his time the going rate had varied between two and fourteen guineas, and was now eight. Grainger quoted eight and a half guineas; Green nine.

J.H. Green, who taught surgery and anatomy at St Thomas's Hospital, was asked in regard to the body-snatchers if it was not 'a distressing thing' to gentlemen of character and education to be obliged to have recourse to persons of this description for obtaining the necessary means of giving instruction to their pupils. 'Certainly,' Mr Green responded predictably to this leading question, 'it really made me for some years, when I had the immediate conducting of the business, I may say quite unhappy.'

Other eminent medical men also impressed on the Committee the general opinion that it was 'a great hardship on men of character and education that they should be able to obtain the means of instruction only by a violation of the law.' They pointed out that many English students were nowadays going to Paris, where the teaching of anatomy had no problems with the laws of the country, and no shortage of subjects. Brodie's assistant, Dr James Somerville, said that exhumation was considered 'a very heinous offence' in France, and was unheard of for anatomical purposes.

Doctors referred to the increasing difficulty of obtaining subjects from Ireland, owing to the opposition of Irish anatomists who wanted all available bodies for themselves. One witness said that the poor in Ireland, having 'waked' a body, would readily part with it for a small sum, but R.D. Grainger added that very few bodies imported from Ireland arrived in a fit state to be dissected. Dr Granville Sharp Pattison told the Committee that bodies were so scarce now in Glasgow that they were 'salted in the summer and hung up and dried like Yarmouth herrings'. He recalled indignantly how he had been tried 'like a common criminal in Edinburgh, a man sitting on each side of me with a drawn bayonet.'

Thomas Wakley of the *Lancet*, a zealous agitator on behalf of provincial and independent anatomists, was able to persuade the Committee that the Royal College of Surgeons tended to favour the London hospital surgeons at the expense of others, however well qualified they might be, and pressed for reform in this

direction as well. (Warburton, in fact, chaired a further
Select Committee in 1834 to enquire into the condition
of medical education and practice, and Sir Astley
Cooper once again headed the list of witnesses,
speaking with obvious prejudice against the quality of
medical education in the provinces.)

Three professional resurrection men were inter-
viewed by the Committee, having been given immunity
from prosecution and protected from identification by
the use of initials – A.B., C.D. and F.G. One naturally
wonders why the third was not E.F. Was it just
carelessness, or was E.F. for some reason thought too
risky – too close to the man's real name, perhaps? A.B.
is generally thought to have been Ben Crouch, the
corpse-king (retired), but I am not completely convinced that it was he.[19] Asked if grave-robbing was a
business worth following, he replied: 'Yes, it is worth
following, if you can get subjects; a man may make a
good living at it, if he is a sober man, and acts with
judgment, and supplies the schools; but that is now out
of his power; there is so much difficulty.' A.B.
contradicted the earlier opinion about the Irish, saying
they cared more for their dead than the English. (It is
certainly true that the Irish were prominent in the
battles which had formerly taken place to save
criminals' corpses from the surgeons after the
executions at Tyburn.)

C.D. is thought to have been Joshua Naples, chiefly
on the grounds that he kept a record of his dealings.
The following exchange occurred between this witness
and the Committee:

Q. Will you state to the Committee what was the
    number of subjects you supplied to the anatomy
    schools in 1809 and 1810?
A. The number in England was, according to my

book, 305 adults, 44 small subjects under three
feet; but the same year, there were 37 for
Edinburgh and 18 we had on hand that were
never used at all.

Q.   Now go to 1810 and 1811?
A.   312.
Q.   Adults for that year?
A.   Yes, and 20 in the summer, 47 small.
Q.   1811 to 1812?
A.   360 in the whole, 56 small ones, these are the
     Edinburgh ones and all.
Q.   Go to 1812 and 1813?
A.   The following summer there were 234 adults, 32
     small ones.
Q.   At what price, on the average, were those
     subjects delivered?
A.   4 guineas adults, small ones were sold at so
     much an inch.[20]

F.G. was asked whether the bodies exhumed consisted
principally of rich or poor, and answered: 'Both classes;
but we could not obtain the rich so easily, because they
were buried so deep.'

James Glennon, a former parish officer, reckoned
there were around two hundred professional body-
snatchers in London:

Q.   Have you heard that to destroy the work of
     another, they go to the churchyard and leave the
     coffin standing upright?
A.   Yes; I have known them fight in the graves.

Joshua Brookes recalled the case of a young woman
who had died from a diseased jaw. Resurrection men
decapitated the exhumed corpse and took away only
the head, leaving the bloody trunk exposed on the

ground, to be found by some labourers going to work next morning. A reward had been offered for the apprehension of these culprits, but they were never caught.

Samuel Twyford, a magistrate, was asked if he thought that, if the 'doing away with exhumation were to be the concomitant of any new plan for obtaining the supply of bodies,' it would tend to 'reconcile the public mind to the change.' 'Certainly,' he answered. 'It is a choice between two evils; it is not difficult to show, that the present evil of exhumation, as now obliged to be conducted, is the greater.'

Richard Spike, a vestryman of the parish of St James, told the Committee that it had been the practice in the parish for several years to allow those who died in the infirmary to be examined by the parish surgeons. He did not think any opposition to the practice would arise. 'It has certainly always struck me,' he said, 'that generally when dead, their friends do not care what becomes of them.' John Abernethy, the lecturer at St Bartholomew's, concurred in this view. He did not believe the feelings of the public would be outraged by making the unclaimed poor available for dissection.

It was clearly the indignity of dissection, rather than mere disturbance of the grave, that gave rise to most of the public's anger. Whilst the Select Committee was in session, the St Katharine Dock was under construction in London, and the human remains from the former St Katharine's churchyard were used to fill up old reservoirs. The use of such remains as mere rubble did not arouse half the offence and agitation provoked by the resurrection men, though of course the latter violated the bodies of those only recently deceased and still close to the hearts of friends and relatives.

Meanwhile, out in the streets, it was business as usual. At the Spring Assizes at Lancaster, Edward Hall, a surgeon, and John Davies, a medical student, were indicted with others for conspiring to secure the body of Jane Fairclough, which had been stolen from a Baptist burial ground at Appleton, Cheshire, in October 1827, and found later in the back yard of a Warrington physician named Moss. Dr Moss explained that he had merely provided facilities to Davies for dissection to be carried out on his premises, and no charges were brought against him. Likewise Hall was merely an intermediary. Davies and a stationer's apprentice of seventeen, named Blundell, who had helped Davies carry the corpse, were charged with possessing a body knowing it to have been illegally disinterred, and were fined twenty pounds and five pounds respectively.

The fury of the public at the existing state of affairs was demonstrated in Glasgow in August, when a medical attendant was seen parcelling up the body of a baby he had assisted in delivering. The observers raised the hue and cry, and an angry mob gave chase, caught the culprit, and would have lynched him on the spot if left to their own devices. He was a student, assisting at the birth, and it was stated on his behalf that the mother had agreed that he could have the body if the child were stillborn, which it was. This business, though clearly signalling the strength of feeling about body-snatching in Scotland, was passed over by the national press as a little local disturbance; as was an incident at Carlisle when the friends of a man hanged there took revenge on two surgeons who had dissected him. One was shot in the face and the other thrown over the parapet of a bridge into the river, to his death.

The report of Warburton's Select Committee was published in July 1828, and concluded: 'To neglect the practice of dissection would lead to the greatest aggravation of human misery, since Anatomy, if not learned by that practice, must be learned by mangling

mangling the living.' In this the powerful voice of Sir
Astley Cooper was distinctly echoed. The· report
revealed to the public officially for the first time the vast
and alarming extent of the resurrectionists' activities,
and urged that something should be done without
delay to stop them. But in spite of widespread public
disquiet and the anxiety in medical circles, the report
was shelved and nothing happened.

Edinburgh, however, was about to blast the
government's apathy with an explosion of outrage, the
fuse of which had already been lit whilst Warburton's
committee was in session.

Chapter V: Death in Edinburgh

'And forbye, I've no notion to take a dram wi' you and wake up the morn on a marble table, wi' Dr Knox fumbling among my tripes. Eh? Ha, Ha!'

James Bridie
The Anatomist, 1930

I overheard in a pub once a conversation between two men standing near the bar. They were talking about murder, and eventually the names of Burke and Hare were mentioned. One of the men turned to a third sitting at the bar. 'You've 'eard of Burke an' 'Are, ain't you, Nobby?' 'No,' he muttered. 'Comics, was they?' This produced a guffaw from his friend. 'Comics, 'e sez! Did y'ear 'im? 'E sez was Burke an' 'Are comics! Oh yes, they was bleedin' comics all right. Dug up dead bodies, didn't they!'

In fact, both men were wrong, but the latter's mistake is very common. There is no evidence whatever that either Burke or Hare ever had anything to do with digging up a dead body, and they were not, therefore, resurrection men, though they are frequently described as such. Indeed, Burke denied that he was a grave-robber so emphatically as to suggest that he would have been ashamed to stoop to such skull-duggery! They cannot be omitted from a book dealing with that business, however, because their activities were in no small measure responsible for ruining the body-snatching trade. The story has been told many times before, with varying degrees of inaccuracy and fanciful elaboration, and I shall confine my account to the bare facts as far as they can be ascertained. It is important to state at the outset that much of the story is based on the confessions made by Burke, whom we might reasonably suspect of being an unreliable witness.

William Burke was the son of an Irish labourer, and was born in 1792 near Strabane. He came to Scotland as a navvy around 1818, working on the canal linking Edinburgh with the Forth and Clyde Canal, and leaving his wife and family in Ireland. It was a time when a continuous stream of poverty-stricken Irish immigrants came to the large industrial towns of Britain seeking work as unskilled labourers. They usually formed close communities noted for their heavy drinking and for being the 'lowest, dampest, dirtiest, most unhealthy and ruinous' in the towns where they settled. In the slums of London, Edinburgh and other large urban centres, they were notorious for their habit of taking in sub-tenants, unhealthily overcrowding their lodgings, and for their 'wakes', when they would allow corpses to lie on beds for several days whilst money was collected for their funerals.

Burke soon took up with a woman named Helen McDougal, who had two children, and he was excommunicated when he refused the local priest's advice to leave her and return to his wife and family. Burke drank heavily and on occasion physically assaulted McDougal, but they stayed together, living in a variety of apartments until 1827, when they moved into a house in Tanner's Close, Edinburgh, on the south side of Castle Mound, with William Hare and his common-law wife Mary.

Hare was also in Irishman, who had likewise come to Scotland as a navvy on the Union Canal, and had settled with Mary after the death of her first husband, who had been Hare's landlord at one time. The squalid lodging house in Tanner's Close – one floor of a slum tenement – thus became Hare's, and as it had several beds, he was able to earn enough money for drink without working for it. He charged his lodgers threepence a night, and they sometimes slept three to a bed. He was a quarrelsome and brutal man, and his wife, who was nicknamed 'Lucky', was evidently a match for him.

Professor John Wilson, who wrote under the pseudonym 'Christopher North', saw both men in prison later and gave us the most reliable descriptions of them. Burke, he wrote, was a 'neat little man of about five feet five … a very active, but not a powerful man, and intended by nature for a dancing master'. He was a 'good specimen of the Irish character – not quarrelsome, expert with the spade, and a pleasant enough companion over a jug of toddy. Nothing repulsive about him, to ordinary observers at least, and certainly not deficient in intelligence.' But he was also impenitent, deceitful and callous. Hare, on the other hand, was 'the most brutal man ever subjected to my sight, and at first look seemingly an idiot'. His hideous features inspired 'disgust and abhorrence, so utterly loathsome was the whole look of the reptile. Sluggish and inert, but a heavier and more muscular man above than Burke.'[1]

One of Hare's lodgers in 1827 was an old soldier named Donald, who died towards the end of the year, owing Hare four pounds in rent. According to Burke, he died of dropsy. It seems that Hare had the idea of selling the body to a surgeon, and needing assistance,

offered Burke a share of the proceeds in return for his
help. Burke agreed, and together they removed Donald
from his coffin (Hare 'unscrewing the nails' according
to Burke's confession), and filled it with tanner's bark,
readily available from the tanning yard close to the
house. In the evening they went to Surgeons' Square,
where six extra-mural lecturers were holding their
courses at this time, among whom were Liston, Monro
and Robert Knox. Burke and Hare had heard of Dr
Monro, and asked some students to direct them to his
rooms. The students, however, were pupils of Dr Knox,
and guessing the men's errand, they directed them to
No. 10, diverting the suppliers for their own benefit.

Burke made a nervous approach to the students who
received him at this address, and he was advised to
bring the body later that night, when it would be
examined and, if it was considered a suitable subject,
paid for. Knox himself examined the corpse when they
brought it in a sack, and paid seven pounds and ten
shillings for it, of which Hare got four pounds and five
shillings and Burke three pounds and five shillings,
with the ominous and irresponsible invitation to call
again when they had another body to dispose of. One
of the students involved in this negotiation later became
Sir William Fergusson, FRS, President of the Royal
College of Surgeons, inventor of surgical instruments
and author of *A System of Practical Surgery*.

Soon after this profitable enterprise, Hare met an old
woman, Abigail Simpson, who was drunk and ill, and
invited her back to his place for a wee dram. After much
conversation and more drink with her hosts, Abigail
accepted their invitation to spend the night there, since
she was too drunk to go home. She awoke next
morning vomiting and begging to be taken home to her
daughter, but by the light of day Burke and Hare
summoned up the courage which had deserted them

the night before. Hare clapped one hand over the old woman's mouth and with the other held her nose, whilst Burke lay over her to stop her thrashing about and making a noise. The woman died within minutes, and they stripped the body and bundled it into a box. They were successful in selling the corpse to Dr Knox, who approved of its freshness, asked no questions, and paid ten pounds.

At this point Robert Knox could, with his Hippocratic oath uppermost in his mind, have saved a number of lives. It was immediately obvious to him that the body had not, like most of those he received, come from the grave, and a few questions would have aroused his own and his students' suspicions as to the cause of death. But if Knox did entertain any suspicions, he never voiced them, and his failure to arrest the activities of Burke and Hare at the outset cost several people of both sexes, both young and old, their lives. That number is generally accepted to have been sixteen, but that is only on the evidence of Burke, and it might have been more. Knox's unquestioning acceptance of Abigail Simpson's corpse told Burke and Hare that there was a lucrative business which was less trouble than digging up bodies from churchyards and more certain of good prices because, from the anatomist's point of view, the fresher bodies were, the better.

The two Irishmen lost little time in pursuing their new careers. One morning in April 1828 William Burke met two young women in a public house. Their names were Mary Paterson and Janet Brown, and though only in their late teens, they were already well-known Edinburgh prostitutes. Burke bought them drinks and cajoled them into going to what he called his lodgings. In fact he took them to the house of his brother, where they were given breakfast by Burke's sister-in-law. Burke's brother went off to work, and Burke gave the

girls a bottle of whisky each, Mary Paterson drinking so
readily that she soon fell asleep. Soon afterwards, Helen
McDougal turned up and found Burke fumbling about
with Janet Brown on the bed. There was an explosive
row during which Burke threw a glass at McDougal and
cut her forehead. Meanwhile, his sister-in-law had
rushed from the house and returned with Hare, and
Janet Brown had left in terror. While Burke's paramour
and his sister-in-law were outside, Burke and Hare
dealt with Mary Paterson as they had with Abigail
Simpson.

Janet Brown came back twice, looking for her friend,
whilst the dead body was still in the room, lying on the
bed and covered with a sheet or blanket. Brown was
persuaded, however, that Paterson had gone off with
Burke. Within a few hours of Mary Paterson's death,
Burke and Hare had stripped the corpse, stuffed it into
a tea chest, and carried it to Surgeons' Square. On duty
at Dr Knox's lecture room, William Fergusson and
another student inspected the corpse with more than
usual interest, both thinking they recognized the
subject. Moreover, Mary Paterson had evidently been a
very attractive girl, though one would hardly think so to
judge by one of the contemporary prints of her. 'The
body,' wrote Knox's biographer (who was his pupil at
the time) 'could not fail to attract attention by its
voluptuous form and beauty'. The two students asked
Burke to cut off the girl's hair, which still had curling
papers in it, handing him a pair of scissors for the
purpose, and then paid eight pounds for the body,
apparently being satisfied with Burke's explanation that
he had purchased this corpse from an old woman living
behind Canongate, after the girl had died of drink.

Knox himself was sufficiently impressed by this
body's freshness and physical perfection to preserve it
in spirits for a period, during which he used it to

illustrate lectures on muscular development and invited an artist to draw the body. It was not dissected for about three months.

There is much contradiction between the various statements made by Burke about the order in which they murdered their acknowledged victims, and it is impossible now to establish the precise chronology of their actions. It is quite possible that two or three of their other victims preceded Mary Paterson to Surgeons' Square, and one who seems most likely to have done so was an old miller named Joseph, who was lodging in Hare's house. He was said to have become very ill with what Hare and his wife feared, or at any rate gave out, to be an infectious disease. Perhaps this story was only meant to explain his sudden disappearance, but in any case, the two men smothered him with a pillow and sold his body to Dr Knox, apparently for ten pounds.

Another of Hare's lodgers was a man of about forty from Cheshire, so Burke said, who was ill with jaundice when they disposed of him in the same way, again for ten pounds. Burke said in one of his confessions that he and Hare had a 'contract' with Knox whereby they received eight pounds in summer and ten pounds in winter, and subsequent events seem to bear this out. It is because Burke said they got eight pounds for Mary Paterson that one suspects she was, in fact, one of their first victims. Her murderers would surely have argued, with a little more experience behind them, that such a prize specimen was worth ten pounds, especially in April. It seems likely that Paterson was sold before the understanding with Knox had become well established.

Poor old women and prostitutes were the easiest prey for Burke and Hare. In the Edinburgh slums of the time, the women drank heavily and were easily enticed by free drink into accompanying one of the men to the lair where most of them were murdered. One old woman was brought home by 'Lucky' Hare and plied with drink until the master of the house came home and smothered her; and Burke murdered another old woman by himself. Both men took part in killing an old cinder woman named Effie. She was murdered in a stable Hare owned, after being plied with drink.

When the two men worked together, which was most of the time, their method was always more or less the same: one man held the body down while the other caused death by suffocation. There was no blood, little noise, and no marks were left on the body. 'When they kept the mouth and nose shut a very few minutes,' one of Burke's dictated statements recorded, 'they could make no resistance, but would convulse and make a rumbling noise in their bellies for some time; after they had ceased crying and making resistance, they left them to die of themselves; but their bodies would often move afterwards, and for some time they would have long breathings before life went away.'

Burke and Hare continued their operations with an old woman and her grandson, a deaf mute. The woman was killed in the usual way after being given whisky. In the case of the boy, Burke said afterwards that he, too, had been suffocated, and there is no real reason to doubt this, despite a later story that Burke had taken the boy across his knee and broken his back. Both bodies were stripped and stuffed into a herring barrel, and an attempt was made to convey this to Surgeons' Square on a cart pulled by a horse which Hare had bought, but the old nag would not pull it, despite being lashed and beaten. Later Hare shot the horse in the tanner's yard and the animal was found to have two old wounds which had been stuffed with cotton and covered with skin to prevent discovery by the purchaser. (If this scene had occurred in England, there would probably have been more sympathy for the horse than for the boy and his grandmother!)

Burke took charge of a drunken old woman found sitting on a stair by a policeman who thought she would be better off in a cell for the night. Saying that he would see her to her lodgings, Burke took the old woman instead to Hare's house, where he and his partner murdered her and then sold the body for ten pounds. Then there was a washerwoman, Mrs Ostler or Hostler, whom Burke and Hare murdered in the house of one Broggan, where she had gone to do some washing. Broggan and his wife were not present. The woman was holding ninepence-halfpenny in her hand when she died, and it was gripped so tightly that her killers had difficulty in prising this bonus from the dead woman, but having done so they put the corpse in a box and hid it in a coal-house until it was convenient to deliver it to Dr Knox. Some time after this, Burke and McDougal moved out of Hare's house and into Broggan's. Some distrust was growing between the two partners.

The reckless daring of Burke and Hare was increasing almost daily, it seems, as they made easy money with no questions asked. After relieving a policeman of his charge and killing a woman in someone else's house, they felt no compunction about disposing of a distant relative, even though she was young and married. Ann McDougal was a cousin of Helen McDougal's former husband, and she came on a visit to Edinburgh, perhaps by invitation, perhaps not. After a few days, Burke and Hare set upon her one afternoon and soon had her stripped and packed for market. A Mrs Haldane and her daughter Peggy were added to the grim catalogue when they became Hare's lodgers. Both were suffocated whilst drunk.

There is no doubt that both Burke's and Hare's

women knew exactly what was going on, although they were never actually present at the killings, retiring discreetly to another room. It was claimed that, whilst 'Lucky' Hare was an accessory before, during and after the fact in many of the murders, Helen McDougal was under the impression merely that Burke and Hare were resurrection men. This is very hard to swallow, particularly when we know that a relative of hers suddenly vanished within a few days of her arrival and other relatives made fruitless enquiries about her. Nevertheless, it seems that the Hares did not trust McDougal, and Mrs Hare actually suggested to Burke that he should murder her. He refused.

Next on the list was a well-known Edinburgh character, James Wilson, a mentally deficient youth of eighteen known to everyone as 'Daft Jamie'. His father was dead and he refused to live with his mother, preferring to wander about the streets and sleep wherever he could. He never wore shoes, and his feet were recognizably deformed. One day Hare's wife brought Jamie home with her, apparently under the pretence that she knew where his mother was, after Jamie had enquired about her. Hare was already at home, and Burke soon arrived on the scene, by which time Jamie was already feeling sleepy as a result of the whisky the Hares had given him. Eventually he lay down on a bed, and Mary Hare having made herself scarce, the two men waited for the young man to fall asleep, aware that he was physically stronger than most of their victims. Soon, however, one of them lost patience (Burke said it was Hare: Hare said it was Burke), and fell upon him. Jamie instantly came to and fought for his life, while one of the murderers just looked on until he was berated by his struggling partner. Both men then overpowered Jamie and succeeded in killing him by their well-tried method.

Having emptied his pockets and stripped him of his few clothes, they duly delivered his body to 10 Surgeons' Square, where they were paid ten pounds. Usually, Burke and Hare burnt the clothes of their victims, but on this occasion, Burke gave Jamie's clothing to his brother's children. Both the clothing and, of course, Jamie's body were subsequently recognized, but no questions appear to have been asked of Burke and Hare who, by this time, flushed with success, were seriously thinking of expanding their services to science.

It seems they were on the point of entering into an agreement with a third party, whom some believed to be Knox's assistant David Paterson, whereby Burke and the third man would go either to Glasgow or to Ireland and supply bodies to Hare in Edinburgh for him to dispose of. If true, this plan seems like a curious reversal of roles, for all the evidence suggests that Hare was the readiest killer and Burke the salesman, using his Irish charm to ingratiate himself with his customers while Hare remained in the background. Be that as it may, the plan was frustrated by other events.

On 31 October 1828, Burke was in a corner shop when a frail old Irish woman came in. Burke learned that her name was Mary Docherty. She had come to Edinburgh looking for her son. As it was early in the morning, Burke invited his compatriot to breakfast, and took her to Broggan's former house, where he and McDougal were still living, along with their lodgers, a Mr Gray and his wife and child. Telling the Grays that Mrs Docherty was a relative of his mother's, Burke persuaded them to move to Hare's lodgings for a night or two so that Mrs Docherty could stay with him during her brief stay in Edinburgh. The coast was thus clear for the disposal of Mrs Docherty. That evening, Hallowe'en, Burke, Hare and their women entertained the

new arrival with whisky and songs until she was in a fit
state to be easily snuffed out, and Mary Hare and Helen
McDougal left the men to get on with the job. When
Mrs Docherty was dead, Burke undressed her and they
laid the body beside the bed, covered with straw. Burke
then went to see Paterson at Dr Knox's premises to tell
him there would be a subject ready for him in the
morning. The four then continued their Hallowe'en
party with the corpse lying on the floor nearby.

Next morning Burke, with a carelessness defying
belief, went round to Hare's house and, full of
solicitude for his inconvenienced lodgers, persuaded
them to return with him for breakfast. Naturally, they
were not long in noticing that the old woman for whom
they had moved out was not present, and Burke told
them that he had turned her out for impudence. A
witness later said that McDougal had told her that she,
McDougal, had 'kicked the damned bitch's backside out
of the door' for being too free with William. Eventually
Mrs Gray, smoking a pipe and dressing her child, began
looking round for a missing stocking, and went close to
the straw beneath which Docherty's corpse still lay. She
then looked under the bed to find some potatoes, much
to the evident agitation of Burke, who began splashing
whisky about the room. At length the Grays were left
alone for a few minutes, and suspecting something
wrong, lifted up the straw to reveal the naked corpse of
an old woman, with blood about the mouth and head.

The horrified couple prepared to leave immediately,
and Gray met McDougal on the stairs. She told Gray
and his wife that the old woman had died of drink,
pleaded with them not to say anything, and tried to
bribe them into remaining silent. Soon she was joined
by Mrs Hare in these entreaties, but to no avail. Gray
made his way to the police office to report his suspicion
of a murder. Meanwhile, Burke and Hare had returned,

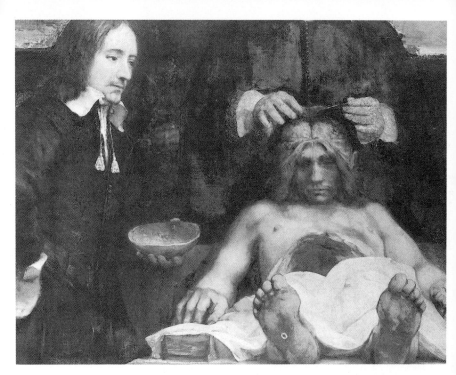

Above: The Anatomy Lesson of Dr Johannes Deijman by Rembrandt, 1656. Much of this painting was destroyed by fire in 1723, but the central part remains, showing the dissected corpse of Joris Fonteyn, who had been hanged for theft. (Rijksmuseum, Amsterdam)

Right: The Reward of Cruelty by Hogarth, 1750. In Britain the bodies of executed murderers were frequently handed over to surgeons for dissection. Hogarth's etching was intended to expose the barbarity of the times, but soon after it was done, the law decreed that *all* murderers' bodies should be 'anatomized'. (Mansell Collection)

THE REWARD OF CRUELTY.

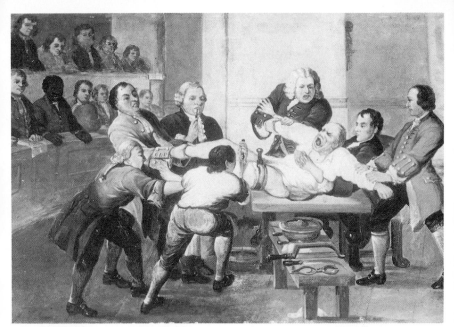

Amputation of a leg at the thigh. This graphic drawing leaves no room for doubt about the importance of a thorough knowledge of anatomy for surgeons. Before the discovery of anaesthesia, speed was of the essence. (By kind permission of the Royal College of Surgeons)

Haworth churchyard, West Yorkshire. It was 'so filled with graves', Charlotte Brontë wrote, 'that the rank weeds and coarse grass scarce had room to shoot up between the monuments'. It was typical of the state of overcrowded graveyards in the early nineteenth century. (Photograph: Rita Bailey)

Right: The Resurrectionists by Rowlandson. This contemporary water-colour captures some of the ghastly spirit of the business well enough, but only the early amateurs would have dug up the entire coffin. (By kind permission of the Royal College of Surgeons)

Below: The 'resurrection stone' at Pannal, North Yorkshire. One of the earliest precautions against body-snatchers was to lower a huge stone like this over the coffin. Too heavy to be lifted by two or three men, it could be removed by block-and-tackle when the grave was safe from disturbance, and used again. (Photograph: Ralph Brooke)

Iron mort-safes in Greyfriars churchyard, Edinburgh. Enclosing graves in heavy iron cages like this was an alternative form of defence. They were often moved from one grave to another, being hired out by the week. (By courtesy of Edinburgh City Libraries)

The 'body-snatchers cage' at Henham, Essex. Iron mort-safes were less common in England than in Scotland (where they were invented), but this one remains in a village churchyard susceptible, no doubt, to visits by London resurrection men. (Photograph: Rita Bailey)

Above: Frenchay, Avon. The heavy stone slab on top of this grave in the churchyard is bolted down in what was obviously a private arrangement, not intended to be hired out to anyone else, even when the corpse was safe. (Photograph: Rita Bailey)

Right: Sir Astley Paston Cooper, Bart. Elected President of the Royal College of Surgeons in 1827, and Vice-President of the Royal Society in 1830, one of his less flattering titles was 'King of the Resurrectionists'. (By kind permission of the Royal College of Surgeons)

Parish reward, Bristol. This poster offering a reward for information leading to the conviction of body-snatchers appeared in Bristol in 1819 after a woman's body was taken from St Augustine's churchyard. (Bristol Record Office, in the collection of Bristol Royal Infirmary)

Watch tower in New Calton Burial Ground, Edinburgh. The three-storey castellated tower was one of the most elaborate of the buildings erected during the body-snatching period to facilitate constant guarding of fresh graves. (Royal Commission on Ancient Monuments, Scotland)

Warblington, Hampshire. A small watch-hut of flint and brick, one of two erected in the parish churchyard, at opposite corners. (Photograph: Rita Bailey)

ANATOMY
AND
Physiology.

DR KNOX, F.R.S.E. *(Successor to* DR BARCLAY, *Fellow of the Royal College of Surgeons and Conservator of its Museum,)* will commence his ANNUAL COURSE OF LECTURES ON THE **ANATOMY AND PHYSIOLOGY** of the Human Body, on Tuesday, the 4th November, at Eleven A. M. His Evening COURSE OF LECTURES, on the same Subject, will commence on the 11th November, at Six P. M.

Each of these Courses will as usual comprise a full Demonstration on fresh Anatomical Subjects, of the Structure of the Human Body, and a History of the Uses of its various Parts; and the Organs and Structures generally, will be described with a constant reference to Practical Medicine and Surgery.

FEE for the First Course, £3, 5s.; Second Course, £2, 4s.; Perpetual, £5, 9s.

N. B.—*These Courses of Lectures qualify for Examination before the various Colleges and Boards.*

PRACTICAL ANATOMY
AND
OPERATIVE SURGERY.

DR KNOX'S ROOMS FOR **PRACTICAL ANATOMY** AND **OPERATIVE SURGERY,** will open on Monday, the 6th of October, and continue open until the End of July 1829.

Two DEMONSTRATIONS will be delivered daily to the Gentlemen attending the Rooms for PRACTICAL ANATOMY. These Demonstrations will be arranged so as to comprise complete Courses of the DESCRIPTIVE ANATOMY of the Human Body, with its application to PATHOLOGY and OPERATIVE SURGERY. The Dissections and Operations to be under the immediate superintendance of DR KNOX. Arrangements have been made to secure as usual an ample supply of Anatomical Subjects.

FEE for the First Course, £3, 5s.; Second Course, £2, 4s.; Perpetual, £5, 9s.

N. B.—*An Additional Fee of Three Guineas includes Subjects.*

*** *Certificates of Attendance on these Courses qualify for Examination before the Royal Colleges of Surgeons, the Army and Navy Medical Boards, &c.*

EDINBURGH, 10. SURGEONS' SQUARE.
25th September 1828.

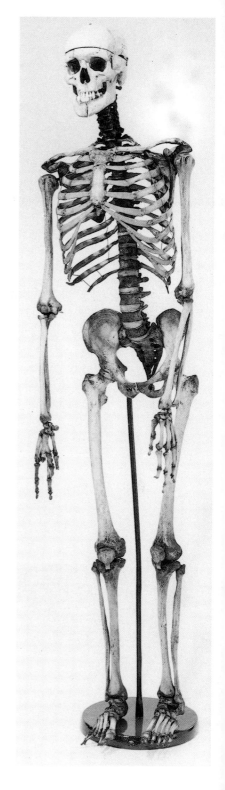

Above: Bill for Dr Knox's course of lectures for the autumn and winter season of 1828-9 at 10 Surgeons' Square, Edinburgh. Note that an 'ample supply of Anatomical Subjects' was promised. (Department of Anatomy, Edinburgh University)

Right: The remains of William Burke. The skeleton of the notorious murderer was preserved after his execution and dissection in 1829. Note the sawn-off skull. (Department of Anatomy, Edinburgh University)

Dr Robert Knox. A rare photograph of Knox, showing him lecturing in his fiftieth year, long after the Burke and Hare scandal. (Courtesy of the Royal College of Surgeons of Edinburgh)

Elizabeth Ross or Cook. This drawing by W.H. Clift was made when the corpse was delivered to the Royal College of Surgeons after her execution for murder in 1832. The woman was reputed to be a body-snatcher. (By kind permission of the Royal College of Surgeons)

unaware of this commotion, and had stuffed the body into a box and instructed a street porter to carry it to Surgeons' Square. There Paterson paid them five pounds on account, the rest to be paid when Dr Knox had seen the body and approved the purchase.

Mr Gray, having made his report to the police, accompanied Sergeant Fisher and Constable Finlay back to Burke's house. They found traces of blood on the bed and the straw, and their enquiries about the old woman were answered by Burke and McDougal with contradictory statements. The sergeant decided to arrest the couple, and later that night a police doctor and a superintendent also inspected the blood stains in Burke's apartment.

Next morning, Sergeant Fisher gained access to the cellar of Dr Knox's premises, and found the body of an old woman in a chest. Gray identified the body as that of the woman he had seen in Burke's house. The police then arrested Hare and his wife. But doctors examining the corpse of Mrs Docherty were unable to say with certainty that she had met her death by violence, and the Lord Advocate could not take the case to court and hope to get a conviction with the circumstantial evidence he had.

Burke and McDougal made further contradictory statements to the Sheriff, giving fantastic accounts of how the old woman happened to be found naked and dead under a heap of straw in their house. Hare, meanwhile, agreed to turn King's Evidence, on being assured that he and his wife would be granted immunity from prosecution in connection with any of the murders he testified about. This was the only course the Lord Advocate felt to be open to him if he wished to bring *any* of the four prisoners to justice.

William Burke and Helen McDougal were committed for trial on Christmas Eve, 1828; Burke for the murder of

Mary Paterson, James Wilson and 'Madgy or Margery, or Mary M'Gonegal or Duffie, or Campbell, or Docherty,' as the indictment read, and McDougal for the murder of the last-named only. There was a lot of confusion about names. Apart from Mrs Docherty's apparent aliases (one witness was asked if the deceased had ever called herself Docherty, and replied, 'Not that I know of'), the old woman herself had called Burke 'Docherty', whilst Mary Paterson had apparently known Burke as 'John'.

The trial opened in the High Court of Justiciary in Edinburgh's Parliament Hall. Police reinforcements controlled the crowds drawn to the square by the high state of public feeling on the issue. The presiding judge was the Lord Justice Clerk, the Right Honourable David Boyle. The Lord Advocate, Sir William Rae, represented the Crown. Burke's defence was led by the Dean of the Faculty, Sir James Moncrieff, and McDougal's by Mr Henry Cockburn.

The proceedings began with a protracted legal argument about the framing of the indictment, defence counsel arguing that the defendants' cases would be prejudiced by a joint trial on different and unconnected charges, and in McDougal's case, by being associated with two murders she was not accused of. The Lord Advocate stated that he had intended McDougal to benefit, not suffer, by being tried jointly with Burke, since if tried separately afterwards she would be faced with substantially the same evidence and her case would be prejudiced; but he would agree not to proceed against her at that time if her counsel so wished it. The judges then ruled that Burke should be tried for each of the three murders separately. The Lord Advocate therefore proposed to proceed with the murder of Mrs Docherty, and to try McDougal at the same time, since she was charged with the same murder in complicity with Burke. To this charge both prisoners pleaded 'Not Guilty', and in accordance with Scottish law, a jury of fifteen men was sworn, consisting mostly of tradesmen and craftsmen from Edinburgh and Leith.

The first witnesses called by the prosecution were those who had seen Mrs Docherty at the Burkes' house, those who had identified her body, and a man who claimed to have heard a woman shouting 'murder', and who demurely explained that he had gone into the street to look for a policeman and, failing to find one, had gone back inside thinking it no longer necessary, as 'the sound had ceased a good deal'. A shop boy testified that Burke had bought a tea chest similar to the one in which Docherty's body was found in Dr Knox's house. A porter named McCulloch testified that he had been hired by Burke to carry a box to Surgeons' Square, and he admitted under pressure that he knew there was a body in it.

David Paterson, presenting himself as 'keeper of the museum belonging to Dr Knox', testified that Burke, McDougal and Mr and Mrs Hare were in the house in Portsburgh when Burke had taken him there to show that he had a subject for sale. Paterson agreed that the appearance of the face and body suggested death by suffocation or strangulation, and spoke about the not-uncommon occurrence of bodies which had not been buried being sold for dissection.

The lodgers, Mr and Mrs Gray, and the police sergeant Fisher, were called to add their testimony to the circumstantial evidence. Mr and Mrs Gray both said that when they had challenged McDougal about the body, she had said it would be worth ten pounds a week to them if they kept quiet. (One wonders if they ever reflected afterwards that, had they been tempted to accept this bribe, they and their child would also have been on Dr Knox's dissecting table in no time.)

The Crown's case clearly rested on the evidence of Hare, and when the informer was called, one of the judges told him that, provided he told the truth without prevarication, he could never afterwards be questioned in a court of justice about the affair, and that he was now called as a witness in the case of Mrs Docherty. 'T'ould woman, sir?' said Hare, as if butter would not melt in his mouth, and he was then sworn on a Catholic Bible.

Hare proved to be a man of few words. His answers were, whenever possible, monosyllabic. He testified that he had known Burke for about a year, and that on 31 October Burke had told him that he had an old woman in his house who would be 'a good shot to take to the doctors'. Hare understood this to mean, he said, that Burke was intent on murdering her. After describing an initial struggle in which Mrs Docherty fell over a stool, Hare told the court that Burke had 'got stride-legs on the top of the woman' and put one hand under her nose and the other over her mouth for ten or fifteen minutes.

'Did she appear dead then?' asked counsel for the prosecution.

'Yes, she appeared dead a wee.'

'Did she appear to be quite dead?'

'She was not moving. I could not say whether she was dead or not.'

'What were you doing all this time?' asked counsel.

'I was sitting on the chair,' said Hare.

'What did he do with the body?'

'He stripped off the clothes. He took it and threw it at the foot of the bed, doubled her up, and threw a sheet over her; he tied her head to her feet.'

When, in cross-examination, McDougal's counsel asked Hare if he had been concerned in supplying subjects to doctors on other occasions than those which had been mentioned, Hare was removed from the dock while a legal argument took place about whether he could be questioned on any matter other than the murder for which the defendants were on trial. The judges ruled that he could be so questioned, but it must be made clear to him that he was not obliged to make any answer that might incriminate him. After this, the following exchange took place between Messrs Hare and Cockburn:

'Were you ever concerned in carrying any other body to any surgeon?'

'I never was concerned about any one but the one that I have mentioned.'

'Now, were you concerned in furnishing that one?'

'No, but I saw them doing it.'

After several questions which Hare declined to answer, Mr Cockburn went on:

'You mentioned, sir, that Burke came and told you that he had got a *shot* for the doctors, and that you understood that that meant that he intended to murder that woman or somebody?'

'That was his meaning.'

'That you understood was his meaning?'

'Yes.'

'How did you understand that? Was that a common phrase amongst you?'

'Amongst him.'

'Not amongst him, but you. Had you ever heard that phrase used by Burke before?'

'Yes.'

'Frequently?'

'Not often.'

'You understood by that, that he was going to murder somebody?'

'He said this many a time when he had no thought of murdering.'

'Then how did you understand that he was going to murder?'

'He told me.'

'Did he tell you whom he meant to murder?'

'Yes.'

'He told you so?'

'Yes.'

After some further questioning about Hare's knowledge of Burke's intent, Mr Cockburn, advising Hare that he was not bound to answer if he did not wish to, asked if he had had several transactions with Dr Knox or his assistants and Burke. 'Do you choose to answer that?'

'No,' Hare replied.

'Had you received money at various times from Dr Knox?'

'I never did.'

'Had you received any money from gentlemen representing themselves as Dr Knox's assistants?'

'Burke might have had it paid to him by Dr Knox, and he could have given it to me.'

'I ask you, did you never receive money from Dr Knox's assistants?'

'No.'

'Who was it that received the money for this old woman's body at Newington?'

'Burke.'

'How much?'

'Five pounds.'

'And you were to get another five pounds on Monday? Did you not say that there was to be five pounds paid to Burke at some other time? Was it five pounds?'

'Yes.'

Mrs Hare, with her child in her arms, who had whooping cough, corroborated her husband's story

with impeccable accuracy. Medical evidence was then
given on the cause of Mrs Docherty's death, the police
surgeon, Alexander Black, and Robert Christison, the
young Professor of Medical Jurisprudence at Edinburgh
University, both testifying that there were grounds for
strong suspicion of a violent death by suffocation or
throttling, but that it was impossible to say with
certainty that this was how the woman had died.

Christison, later Sir Robert, became one of the leading
early figures in forensic medicine, partly through his
meticulous examination of Mrs Docherty's body in this
case and his careful presentation of the evidence. He
soon had a reputation as a lecturer and witness 'far
more logical, accurate and unimpeachable than any
other that had yet appeared.' He put his own life at risk
on more than one occasion in testing the effects of
poisons on himself, and in 1875 became President of the
British Medical Association. He was also well acquaint-
ed with the activities of the grave-robbers, and it is
partly on his evidence that we rely for knowledge of
their methods.

The prosecution having concluded its case, the
defence called no witnesses. There was no appearance
by Dr Knox, whom many considered as guilty as Burke
and Hare. The Lord Advocate, in making his closing
address to the jury, began with the curious observation
that the public's anxiety and alarm, its terror and
dismay at such an atrocious crime, arose from its
detestation of the assassins' deeds, 'and from venera-
tion of the ashes of the dead'. He also pointed out that
Hare, in particular, appeared to be speaking the truth,
and demanded a verdict of guilty against both prisoners
at the bar.

In their defence of Burke and McDougal, Sir James
Moncrieff and Mr Cockburn concentrated their efforts
on attempting to discredit the evidence of Hare, this

'squalid wretch' and 'cold-blooded villain' who had
nothing to lose by including the defendants among his
victims by breaking his oath as he had broken into 'the
bloody house of life', as Mr Cockburn expressed it. The
Dean of Faculty told the jury that Burke and Hare were
body-snatchers, though Hare, 'with his usual
adherence to truth, chooses to deny this unquestion-
able fact', and that they were 'constantly employed by
Dr Knox and others, to procure and sell dead bodies.'
But Burke was not on trial for procuring subjects for
anatomists. Mr Cockburn told the jury, in his address in
defence of McDougal: 'It is impossible to shut one's
eyes to the fact, that this husband was a professional
resurrectionist. His trade consisted in supplying
anatomical teachers with subjects, a trade which, when
conducted properly, is not only lawful, but absolutely
necessary.' Apparently ignorant of the fact that Burke
had a wife living in Ireland, Mr Cockburn referred to
Helen McDougal as Burke's wife by the Scottish law of
conjugal cohabitation, and told the jury: 'To know of an
intended murder, and to conceal it, is not, in law,
equivalent to being the murderer by accession.'

Burke's counsel also emphasized that public horror at
the trade in dead bodies prejudiced Burke's case, and
implored the jury to reach its verdicts purely on the
evidence presented on this single charge. In his
summing-up, the Lord Justice Clerk pointed out that
McDougal's case was not the same as Taylor's in the
case of the murdered baby in 1807, which Mr Cockburn
had cited as authority for his statement, and suggested
to the jury that if they believed the evidence, they must
find McDougal guilty as well as Burke.

The trial had continued through the night, and it was
the morning of Christmas Day when the jurymen
retired to consider their verdicts at half past eight. They
were out for fifty minutes. They found Burke guilty but

the case against McDougal not proven. 'Nelly,' Burke said to her, 'you're out of the scrape.' In setting McDougal free, the Lord Justice Clerk reminded her that she had not been found *not guilty*, and her conscience must draw the proper conclusion as she sought to start a new and better life. Although she was technically free to go, it was thought prudent to keep her locked up for a few days for her own safety.

In proposing the death penalty for Burke, one of their lordships referred to the case as 'one of the most monstrous delineations of human depravity that has ever been brought under your consideration.' The Lord Justice Clerk, black cap on his head, reflected on the advisability of hanging Burke's body in chains after his execution, as a deterrent to others, but considered it more fitting that he should be publicly dissected and anatomized, 'and I trust that if it is ever customary to preserve skeletons, yours will be preserved, in order that posterity may keep in remembrance your atrocious crimes.' The judge then sentenced Burke to be hanged in the Lawnmarket at Edinburgh on 28 January, and his body to be delivered to Dr Alexander Monro, Professor of Anatomy at the university. Their lordships then dispersed for their Christmas dinners.

Whilst there was general public and press satisfaction at the fate of Burke, there was a good deal of disquiet about other aspects of the appalling revelations brought forth in recent days. Not only had McDougal and the Hares got off scot-free, despite their obvious guilt, but no account of how Daft Jamie had met his death had been forthcoming because of the way the trial had been conducted, and no doctors had been called to account for their parts in these hideous affairs. Three days after the trial ended, a gang of youths broke several windows of Dr Knox's house.

Helen McDougal had to be smuggled away from

Edinburgh to save her from being lynched by the mob. In the condemned cell, meanwhile, Burke made a confession to the Sheriff and the Procurator Fiscal, and received visits from both Catholic and Protestant clergymen, one of whom apparently told him that a 'dying man, covered with guilt, and without hope except in the infinite mercy of Almighty God, through our blessed Redeemer the Lord Jesus Christ ... must prepare himself to seek it by forgiving from his heart all who had done him wrong,' and advised him to 'Speak the truth, and nothing but the truth, without any attempt either to palliate his own iniquities, or to implicate Hare more deeply than the facts warranted.' The priest then asked the Irish labourer, according to a newspaper: 'By what means were these fearful atrocities perpetrated?' Burke, however, seems to have been preoccupied in the condemned cell with brooding on the fact that Knox still owed him five pounds.

A detailed confession by Burke was eventually published in the Edinburgh *Courant*. In his various statements, Burke made Hare the chief actor in the drama, intimating that he, Burke, had been brought up in Ireland 'under the influence of religious impressions, and that he was accustomed to read his Catechism and Prayer-book,' but he had been led astray by bad company since coming to Scotland.[2] If we are to believe Burke's statement that he had confessed to all the murders he and Hare committed, it means that sixteen people died in the course of nine months for the sake of less than a hundred and fifty pounds – twelve women, two men and two boys.

A vast and noisy crowd gathered in Edinburgh's Lawnmarket to witness the execution of Burke on 28 January 1829. When the executioner, Williams, drew the bolt, Burke's body was watched by the multitude as it swung on the rope, struggled a little against strangulation, and made convulsive movements until life had expired. After an hour, the body was cut down, and next morning it was taken to the dissecting room of Monro *tertius* where, that afternoon, the professor lectured on it for two hours to an eager audience of ticket-holders, who saw the upper part of Burke's head sawn off to expose the brain.

Next day, enthusiastic visitors were allowed to file past the corpse that had been prepared for exhibition in the medical college. The naked body lay on a black marble table, the head shaved and showing a continuous scar where the skull had been replaced, with signs of blood still on it. More than twenty thousand people, most but not all of them men, were estimated to have viewed the spectacle of Burke's remains, and the hint from the learned judge being taken, his skeleton was preserved at Edinburgh University's Medical School, where it remains to this day.

Among much ludicrous speculation and pseudo-scientific comment on Burke was a phrenologist's opinion that his 'love of approbation' was well developed, and if this were true, and there were life after death, the doctors and the mob gave Burke's ghost the satisfaction of being well rewarded at last, British justice having an infallible instinct for increasing morbid curiosity and depravity by making the punishment even more gruesome and horrific than the original crime. Sir Walter Scott referred to Burke as 'lying in state' at the college. 'The strange means by which the wretch made money,' he wrote, 'are scarce more disgusting than the eager curiosity with which the public have licked up all the carrion details of this business.'[3]

It is not known what became of the other three principals in this drama. 'Lucky' Hare is believed to have returned to Ireland, but of Helen McDougal's subsequent movements we know nothing except that she passed through Newcastle. She is said to have died in Australia in 1868.[4]

As for Hare, there was a great deal of public and press agitation for him to be brought to trial, despite the immunity he had been granted. When it became clear that the authorities were to take no further action, Jamie Wilson's mother attempted unsuccessfully to bring a private prosecution against Hare for the murder of her son. After lengthy legal soul-searching about the propriety of allowing Hare to be hanged through, as it were, a loop-hole in the law, the High Court of Justiciary ruled that the Lord Advocate's handling of the case in the public interest took priority over any private interest, and that Hare had been promised protection from *any* prosecution for the murders.

Hare left Calton Jail under the name of Black, and was put aboard a coach bound for Dumfries, as he would soon have been lynched in Edinburgh. From there it is believed that he crossed the border into England. Legend has it that he was deliberately blinded with quicklime, and ended his days begging at a corner of Oxford Street in London.[5] There is no evidence to support these stories, however, and the probability is that Hare went back to Ireland.

The West Port murders were the talk of Britain long afterwards, and they gave a new verb to the English language – to 'burke', meaning to suffocate. Many broadsides and popular ballads on the crimes were hawked on the streets and eagerly absorbed, though some of the verses were almost worse crimes against humanity than the original offences. For a time, youths in Scottish and some English towns thought it a great joke to leap out at women and girls in the streets and slap sticking-plaster on their mouths, delighting in the terror they caused. The names of Burke and Hare were used by ignorant parents to frighten naughty children into obedience.

The scenes of the murders became Edinburgh's biggest tourist attractions in the nineteenth century, but Tanner's Close was demolished in 1902, and modern buildings now cover the former notorious sites of the Wester Portsburgh district.

Chapter VI: Choice of Evils

'We are anatomists, not policemen; we are scientists, not moralists. Do I, I, care if every lewd and sottish woman of the streets has her throat slit from ear to ear? She served no purpose in life save the cheapening of physical passion and the petty traffics of lust. Let her serve her purpose in death.'

Dylan Thomas
The Doctor and the Devils, 1944

The most important question arising out of the Scottish mass murders was not the fate of the criminals but the future practice of the doctors. Although Dr Knox had been listed as a witness for the prosecution in the Burke trial, he was not called. This was because the charges having been reduced to one – the murder of Docherty, whose body Knox had probably not seen – he could give no useful evidence on that charge.[1] Many people thought he should have been in the dock himself, however, and a few days after Burke's execution a mob burned and hanged an effigy of Knox outside his house in Newington Place.

Dr Knox's role in the appalling business has been debated ever since it came to light. There was no doubt in the minds of local folk who knew of his activities and chanted in the streets of Edinburgh several variations on the same popular theme:

'Up the close and doon the stair,
But and ben wi' Burke and Hare.
Burke's the butcher, Hare's the thief,
Knox the boy who buys the beef.'*

There can be very little reasonable doubt that Knox
knew, or at least suspected, that he was dealing with
murderers, despite the many attempts to clear him of
that suspicion. During 1828, Knox's anatomical classes
attracted nearly five hundred students, the largest
number ever recorded in Britain. Knox would not have
disappointed his expectant classes under any circumstances, and he paid out around eight hundred pounds
to keep up his supply of subjects. There is no evidence
to suggest that he ever gave conscious encouragement
for any criminal act, but he unquestionably turned a
blind eye on the doings of Burke and Hare, indifferent
as to the source of his subjects so long as they kept
coming. He ordered his assistant Paterson not to ask
questions of people who brought bodies for dissection,
and showed signs of guilty agitation over one of the
murderers' victims.

Burke said at the end of one of his confessions that
'Doctor Knox Never incoureged him Nither taught or
incoregd him to murder any person Nether any of his
asistents that worthy gentleman Mr Fergeson was the
only man that ever mentioned any thing about the
bodies He inquired where we got that yong woman
paterson Sined William Burk prisoner.'[2] Nevertheless,
wild rumours exaggerating the scale of both resurrectionists' and murderers' operations led to a conviction in
the public mind that every lecturer in anatomy
employed men like Burke and Hare, and the

* 'But and ben' – Scottish colloquialism for two-room apartment,
also used in the sense of 'in and out'.

disappearance of practically every missing person in Edinburgh was attributed to Burke and his 'gang' and to the evil influence of Dr Knox. One of a series of popular prints entitled 'Noxiana' showed the doctor butchering a pig, with the caption: 'If you can get them when just killed, this is of great advantage.'

Knox himself seemed unperturbed at first by all the press and public attacks on him. An arrogant man who held his fellow anatomists up to ridicule before his students, he once referred obliquely to the surgical operations of his rival Liston as being dependent on 'brute force, ignorance and presumption'. (And indeed, Liston did once, in his haste to cut off a man's leg, also sever two of his assistant's fingers and one of his patient's testicles!)[3]

Disfigured and half blinded by smallpox as a child, Knox was nicknamed 'Old Cyclops', and he compensated for his physical appearance by becoming what Americans call a snappy dresser. He was above medium height and muscular, with powerful shoulders and long arms, and he had a military erectness, with a 'strikingly fine head', as his biographer Lonsdale tells us, 'that shone in all its baldness'. The muscles in his face were restless when his concentration was at its most intense. 'These involuntary twitchings were far from agreeable,' Lonsdale says, 'especially those which affected his underlip, the crossing of which from side to side produced a kind of smacking noise. Co-ordinate or alternating with transfacial movements, the neck was extended, the shoulders raised, and the arm drawn to the side ...' We may suspect, surely, the self-deception and dogmatism of a fanatic.

It is a curious irony that whilst Knox was serving as a young doctor at the Battle of Waterloo, William Burke was also on the battlefield as a medical orderly, though not with his subsequent employer. Did the blood and horror have a brutalizing effect on the man of education and science as well as on the unimaginative labourer?

Knox was, however, a brilliant teacher. He inherited the private anatomy school at 10 Surgeons' Square from his former teacher, Dr Barclay. His advertisement for his 1828–9 course of lectures on practical anatomy and operative surgery stated that 'Arrangements have been made to secure as usual an ample supply of Anatomical Subjects,' and after Burke's trial he told his students, 'I will do just as I have done heretofore.' He had been purchasing corpses from sources other than Burke and Hare, of course, and at the time of Mrs Docherty's murder, Andrew Merrilees sent a note, dated 29 October, which read: 'Doctor am in the east, and has been doin little busnis, an short of siller send out abot aught and twenty shilins way the carer the thing will bee in abot 4 on Saturday mornin its a shusa hae the plase open. And. M – s.'*

David Paterson, Knox's dissecting room assistant, was sacked after the trial for allegedly selling bodies bought for Dr Knox to another anatomist at a higher price. Paterson published a strong denial in which he took his revenge on Knox, stating among other things that the doctor had been sufficiently alarmed by the possibility of Daft Jamie's body being widely recognized as to get Fergusson to cut off the head and feet immediately, and that he had carried out the dissection with more than usual promptness.[4]

Knox wrote a letter to Sir Robert Peel shortly before Burke's arrest, complaining that a consignment of corpses intended for his use had been prevented from sailing from Dublin by an Irish lecturer, apparently out of bloody-mindedness. An assistant had been sent on board the vessel, Knox wrote, who, 'suspecting the

---

* siller – silver or cash;   shusa – a female corpse (Scottish)

boxes to contain subjects, procured a warrant, had them broken open and their contents left exposed on the quay for, as I am informed, the space of two days, apparently for the purpose of irritating the populace and preventing the supply of the schools.' In fact, the lecturers in anatomy at Dublin University *did* have a vested interest in keeping Britain short of subjects in order to attract more students there. But in the circumstances, Knox considered it prudent not to post this letter.

After an initial period when he remained aloof from all the public clamour about him, Knox's equanimity was upset sufficiently for him to announce that he had arranged for ten gentlemen, headed by the Marquis of Queensberry, to investigate his dealings with Burke and Hare and make their findings public. One of the gentlemen invited was Sir Walter Scott, who declined to be involved in what he anticipated would be a whitewash of 'this much to be suspected individual'. The Marquis also resigned from the committee in less than a fortnight, giving no reason for his decision, and John Robinson, Secretary of the Royal Society, became its chairman instead. The other members included Sir George Ballingall, Professor of Military Surgery, James Russell, Professor of Clinical Surgery, and a professor of physic, William Pulteney Alison, who had been listed as a trial witness but, like Knox, had not been called.

The committee took about five weeks to make its report, which was published in the *Edinburgh Evening Courant* on 21 March 1829. Predictably, it cleared Dr Knox of any knowledge or suspicion of murder, and admonished him merely for being a little incautious in entrusting his door-keeper and assistants to purchase corpses without enquiring too closely into their origins. In his arrogance and apparent contempt for the poor, Knox seems to have believed genuinely that 'A considerable supply of subjects for anatomical purposes might be procured by purchase, and without any crime, from the relatives or connections of deceased persons of the lowest ranks of society.' There was, however, the committee pointed out, 'nothing contrary to the law of the land in procuring subjects for dissection in that way.'

Without mentioning Daft Jamie or any victim by name, the report said that it had been proved to the committee's satisfaction that 'No mutilation or disfigurement of any kind was ever practised with a view to conceal the features, or abstract unreasonably any part of the body, the presence of which would have facilitated detection.' The committee was satisfied, also, that none of the bodies purchased from Burke and Hare bore 'any external marks by which it could have been known, whether they had died by violence, or suddenly from natural causes, or from disease of short duration,' and that no suspicion of murder was ever expressed to Dr Knox 'by any one either of his assistants, or of his very numerous class …'

The committee's full report is given as Appendix B. No list of the witnesses it had questioned nor any evidence to support its conclusions was published, and it naturally did little to satisfy public opinion, though the riots and disturbances slowly died down. But Knox's association with Burke and Hare was his downfall. He could not live down the sinister reputation he had acquired. He continued lecturing to enthusiastic students for a time, but his popularity began to wane. He failed to get university appointments he applied for; the Royal Society of Edinburgh struck his name from the roll of its Fellows and his licence to lecture was eventually withdrawn. He moved to Glasgow and then to London, where he wrote textbooks including a best-selling *Manual of Human Anatomy*, and in 1856 took up an appointment as pathological anatomist to the Cancer Hospital. But in 1862 he died, a man ruined by an arrogance which had made him many enemies who were quick to take advantage of his mistakes.

Much print has been expended over the years in attempts to defend Robert Knox, and to present him as an unfortunate scapegoat for the rest of the medical profession engaged in anatomical studies at the time. Even while Knox was still alive, Lord Cockburn, the Scottish judge who as a counsel had successfully defended Helen McDougal, wrote in his memoirs that: 'All our anatomists incurred a most unjust, and a very alarming, though not unnatural odium; Dr Knox, in particular, against whom not only the anger of the populace, but the condemnation of more intelligent persons was specially directed. But tried in reference to the invariable and the necessary practice of the profession, our anatomists were spotlessly correct, and Knox the most correct of them all.' The value of this judgment is perhaps placed in perspective by another of Lord Cockburn's later pronouncements to the effect that 'except that he murdered', William Burke was a reasonable and respectable man![5]

Knox was a man carried away by ambition and zealousness into what amounted to criminal negligence. The question of his possible prosecution as an accessory to murder was obviously raised at some point, but the Edinburgh elite closed ranks to protect the city's intellectual establishment from a damaging presentation of one and perhaps more of its members as public spectacles. His share of the responsibility for more than a dozen murders cannot be shrugged off, however. As Sir Robert Christison wrote long afterwards: 'My own opinion at the time was that Dr Knox ... had rather wilfully shut his eyes to incidents which ought to have excited the grave suspicions of a man of his intelligence.'[6]

Knox may not have encouraged murder directly, but his clear indifference as to the source of his subjects encouraged Burke and Hare to believe they could get away with it. The point is not whether Knox knew he was receiving murder victims, which his apologists so vigorously deny, but that he knew his subjects had not been buried, and ought therefore to have enquired much more closely into their origins. Jesus Christ himself would have been impressed by the rate at which Burke and Hare turned blood into whisky, delivering at least sixteen unburied corpses in the course of about nine months. The young body of Mary Paterson, in which Knox took so much interest in other respects, ought to have aroused his curiosity about the cause of death, even more perhaps than that of Daft Jamie and the older victims. Knox was unfortunate only in the sense that *all* anatomists' dealings with the body-snatchers were potential incitements to murder, and he was the one who got landed with Burke and Hare. Having said all that, however, the chief responsibility for the growing evils lay squarely on the shoulders of the government.

On the same day that the report of Knox's committee was published in Edinburgh, the House of Commons was listening to a Bill presented by Henry Warburton to free anatomists from the absurd restrictions the law placed on them. The Bill was supported by the Lord Advocate for Scotland, Sir William Rae, who had led the Crown's prosecution of Burke and McDougal. Its main proposals were that the bodies of those who died in hospitals and workhouses, if unclaimed after three days, could be disposed of for anatomical examination; that buildings where anatomy lectures were given should be licensed and superintending commissioners appointed; and that the robbing of graves should be made a felony punishable by six months' imprisonment for a first offence and two years for a second. All this was broadly in line with what already happened in many European countries.

During the debates that followed, Sir Astley Cooper's brother (another Bransby), the Member for Gloucester, raised objections of detail on behalf of the Royal College of Surgeons, whose members had become nervous about the effects of reform on their status and privileges. The Member for Norwich took the opportunity to defend Dr Knox against a press accusation of 'intolerable criminality'. Most members feared that an Act which legalized dissection would be unpopular, but most of them also recognized by this time that some action had to be taken to put an end to body-snatching and to prevent a repetition of the Edinburgh scandal. Fears were expressed that the Bill, if it became law, would lead to brutal men selling the bodies of their own children to the surgeons, and one Member even feared that 'in a moment of excitement or intoxication' some men might engage to 'sell their bodies to the Jews'.

The Bill was opposed at the committee stage by the Member for Cambridge, who said that it was a measure which gave over the bodies of the poor and friendless to the surgeons. Joseph Hume, the Member for Aberdeen burghs, who had been a member of the Select Committee, took the opposite view, saying that the measure would benefit the whole community, including the poor. Edward Protheroe, another member of the Select Committee, and the Member for Evesham, said that he had gone into the committee as much prejudiced against it as any man could be, but that the evidence had completely removed that prejudice. Despite general unease about the Bill's terms, Warburton carried it through. The Bill was committed with an instruction, moved by the Member for Oxford

University but opposed by Warburton, that the Act which gave judges the power to order murderers' bodies to be dissected after execution should be repealed at the same time.

It was read a third time and passed by the Commons on 20 May 1829, notwithstanding the opposition of Sir C. Forbes, the Tory Member for Malmesbury, who said he understood friends of the sick in hospital were only allowed to visit them once a week, on Tuesdays – 'So that a husband might enquire after his wife's health on one Tuesday and be told that she was getting well, and on the following Tuesday he might be told that she was dead and dissected.' The Home Secretary, Peel, said the measure was necessary to put a stop to the various atrocities caused by the difficulties of obtaining dead bodies. It was painful, he said, to allude to the recent Edinburgh murders; but he hardly dared to think that those were the only crimes that had sprung out of the system.

Heated debate was going on in the press, too. As far as the London papers were concerned, Edinburgh was a long way off and most of the trouble there was put down by *The Times* to Scottish hooliganism and the unwisdom of magistrates. But horror of dissection and all its accompaniments was both older and stronger in Scotland than in England. The *Aberdeen Journal* pontificated in response to the discovery in the Guestrow there of the limbless body of a man who had been buried at New Deer: 'We had occasion before to caution resurrectionists not to tamper with the present and provoked state of public feeling; for some dreadful and summary mode of punishment will unquestionably overtake those who engage in such wanton and outrageous acts.'

When Warburton's Bill came before the House of Lords for its second reading on 5 June, the Archbishop of Canterbury, William Howley, led the opposition to it, not because he did not sympathise with its objectives, but because he wanted it postponed and amended so as to be 'less offensive to the feelings of the community, and therefore less objectionable.'

Lord Tenterden preferred the status quo, and observed that greater vigilance by doctors in ascertaining whether subjects were victims of violence or had died natural deaths would prevent any recurrence of such crimes as had lately been committed in Edinburgh; and the Earl of Harewood, who must have been either abroad or asleep for some time, delivered himself of the opinion that it was a national disgrace that the recent affairs in Edinburgh had not been more fully investigated and the public properly informed of the facts.

The Bill was supported by Prime Minister Wellington and the Earl of Haddington, the latter pointing out that the dreadful atrocities which had taken place in Edinburgh had in fact been probed to the bottom. The Archbishop won the day, however. There was too much dissatisfaction with the Bill in its present form, and it was withdrawn. One of the powerful public voices against it had been that of Thomas Wakley, who said that it was totally unacceptable if it did not forbid the sale of bodies and abolish the practice of handing the corpses of executed criminals to surgeons.

In Scotland, meanwhile, the public of Aberdeen thought they had facts enough to take the law into their own hands when they stormed Dr Andrew Moir's anatomical theatre, which they had by this time nicknamed the 'burkin' hoose'. Moir had an old reputation as a body-snatcher, and when a dog dug up a human limb on some waste land at the back of the theatre, it soon got around that the ground was littered with dismembered corpses. Certainly Moir's staff had taken insufficient care in disposing of human remains. Soon a huge mob burst into the anatomical theatre, where three corpses were found in the dissecting room, one with the skull removed. While some of the crowd took these bodies away and paraded the ghastly exhibits through the streets of the town, others set fire to the theatre, and yet more smashed the windows of Moir's house in the Guestrow.

Soon the Lord Provost arrived on the scene with magistrates, officers and special constables, and read the Riot Act to a crowd of between ten and twenty thousand people thronging the city's central streets. Troops were also called out, but did not go into action, although the mob prevented firemen from putting out the fire, and the anatomical theatre, not long built, was soon a heap of smouldering rubble. A medical student was saved only at the last minute from being lynched, and Moir himself hid in St Nicholas's churchyard, a place he knew well enough.

Three men were arrested in connection with this trouble and charged with mobbing and rioting, wilful fire-raising and assault. The fire-raising charge – a capital crime – was subsequently dropped, along with that of assault. One of the men, a blacksmith named Sharpe, claimed that he had only gone to the anatomical theatre to see if he could find his grandmother there, as she had been buried only recently. The three were imprisoned for a year, and Moir was compensated by the town to the tune of two hundred and thirty-five pounds. He set up shop elsewhere, while the fickle press raged at what it saw as ludicrously inadequate sentences passed on the criminals.

There was no subsidence in the activities of the resurrection men. Notwithstanding that 1829 was the year in which Peel introduced his police force to the metropolis, in place of the former parish constables who were unable to uphold the law in the face of increasing crime in a new industrial society, London churchyards continued to be hives of nocturnal activity. A man was arrested at Newington with the body of a Mrs Christy in a sack, disinterred from Walworth. A surgeon was arrested just after midnight in the West End with a sack containing a man's body, which he said he had with the widow's permission, in order to determine the cause of death and then return it. Some doubt was thrown on this story when it emerged that the widow in question had been paid four pounds for the body. If she was in league with the body-snatchers, she was not the only woman in the trade, as we have seen and shall see again, but the case was dismissed on condition that the body be buried as soon as the surgeon had finished with it.

A well-known London body-snatcher named Robert Cummings, commonly known as 'Old Bob', was ambushed by police as he drove into London on a cart with some companions. After a thorough search of the cart had revealed nothing suspicious, the men were allowed to go: the police had failed to detect that one of Cummings's companions was a corpse, dressed up and supported by the others.

Tom Vaughan, one of the London body-snatchers whom Sir Astley Cooper had often employed and sometimes got out of trouble, had moved to Devonport in 1830, and was now going under the name of Goslin. He lived in a house close to the parish church at Stoke Damerel, where he and his wife Louisa and three young partners, in league with the local grave-digger, obtained bodies to send to London. The Exeter-to-London stagecoach which William Cobbett admired about this time may sometimes have carried non-paying passengers unsuspected by other travellers, although most of Goslin's subjects were probably sent by sea. It was not many months before the five were arrested, and a search of the house revealed two corpses, a large number of teeth, and a woman's shift.

Tried at the Devon General Sessions at Exeter in December 1830, Goslin and three others got a fortnight in prison for digging up the bodies of Thomas Webb and Eliza Hanger, and seven years' transportation for stealing the shift, valued at six pence and solemnly identified in court as the property, in law, of the vicar, the archdeacon and the Bishop of Exeter. The grave-digger, Nicholas Wood, got twelve months for assisting the gang, and a young woman was acquitted. 'To disinter and carry away a dead body,' said the judge, 'is very properly deemed by the law a gross outrage on the feelings of our nature and punishable as a misdemeanour.' Vaughan then enquired of the judge whether the teeth would be returned to him, as he had not been charged in connection with them. Although he had been in prison many times, and was obviously not one of the most careful operators, the failure to return the shift to the coffin was presumably due to lack of experience on the part of his younger colleagues.[7]

In November of that year, the government of Wellington fell, and with it, of course, Peel's tenure at the Home Office. After the failure of Warburton's Bill, and now this, the teachers of anatomy must have been thoroughly downhearted. Peel had seemed to be the surgeons' best hope of facilitating a change in the law favourable to them.

One of the most notorious of the provincial resurrection men was busy around this period in Yorkshire. John Craig Hodgson was the son of a Leeds cabinet maker and publican, and although he studied medicine in Edinburgh, he did not, apparently, qualify as a doctor, but gained some useful experience in obtaining subjects for dissection. He worked as a solicitor's clerk in his native town during the period of his notoriety, living in a house in Mill Lane which had a coal cellar, accessible from the street, where he was reputed to dump bodies brought from local churchyards until he found customers for them.

Rumour implicates Hodgson in some previously mentioned cases of body-snatching in and around Leeds, but as he was then barely sixteen years old, we may put this down to popular confusion with other local resurrectionists. However, in July 1831 he was arrested and accused of having dug up the body of Thomas Rothery, a dyer who had been scalded to death when he fell into a vat of hot liquid at the dying-mill in Wortley where he was employed. He had been buried on Sunday, 5 June, in the burial ground of the local Episcopal Chapel, and on Thursday night his body vanished from the grave. Hodgson had rather stupidly found a temporary repository for the corpse in the office of his employer, Mr Gaunt, at the corner of Albion Street. At the Leeds Borough Sessions, he was found guilty of a misdemeanour and given six weeks in prison. He was only about twenty years old at this time. He admitted that he had acted in league with a medical man, but refused to divulge the doctor's name.

Eight months later, Hodgson was before the York Assizes charged with conspiracy to disinter a dead body, this time that of a young girl from Ardsley churchyard. A cap and nightgown had been removed from the corpse and left lying on the ground. Hodgson had apparently knocked up an ironmonger in Briggate after the shop had closed and said he was in urgent need of a spade. The ironmonger had obligingly sold him one. This time Hodgson was given a spell in the House of Correction at Wakefield, but he proved incorrigible, at any rate during his time in Leeds. It was said that he facilitated the packing of corpses into boxes by severing the hip-joints, a method familiar enough to other body-snatchers.[8]

England, like Scotland, was moving towards a state of general panic in which every missing person was thought to be lying on a dissecting table somewhere. In London on Saturday, 5 November 1831, the drama finally reached its climax, if not its final curtain, when police were called to King's College by Mr Partridge, the anatomy demonstrator, who said he had three men there trying to sell him the body of a young boy, about which he entertained some suspicions.

Earlier in the day, two of the men, John Bishop and James May, called on the porter, Mr Hill, to offer him a subject for twelve guineas. It was, they said, a male subject of about fourteen years, very fresh, and they could deliver it that afternoon. Mr Hill said he would ask Mr Partridge if he wanted it, and after some haggling, their price was knocked down to nine guineas. Later, the two men came back, and with them were Thomas Williams and a street porter named Shields, carrying a hamper. May was drunk, as indeed he had been in the morning. They opened the hamper and tipped out the corpse on the floor, asking for their money. But Hill was immediately suspicious. It was obvious that the boy's body had not been buried; rigor mortis was still present and there was a deep cut on the forehead with coagulated blood round it. He asked what the boy had died of, but May retorted that that was no business of Hill's. Hill then went to fetch Partridge, who looked at the body and noticed in particular the boy's badly swollen jaw and lips, and bloodshot eyes. Mr Partridge left the room and sent someone for the police, then returned and detained the men by producing a fifty-pound note which he said he would have to get changed. Bishop offered to take a little on account and return for the rest on Monday. May kindly offered to take Partridge's fifty-pound note and get it changed for him. Partridge declined these generous offers, and delayed the men's departure until a police inspector and several constables turned up and arrested all four men.

Asked his trade or profession, Bishop replied truculently, 'I'm a bloody body-snatcher.' The other three denied all knowledge of the matter, Williams (whose real name was Head) claiming that he had only gone to King's College with the others in order to look at the building. He found little scope for his interest in architecture for the next month, after the prisoners were remanded in custody by the magistrate at Bow Street.

Examination of the dead boy's body by three surgeons, including Mr Partridge, led to the conclusion that he had been murdered, although two of them thought death had been caused by a blow on the head from a blunt instrument, while the other considered that this blow had only stunned the boy and that his neck had been dislocated afterwards. Enquiries revealed that the body had previously been offered to Guy's Hospital and Grainger's Anatomical Theatre, but both had declined to purchase it. May had also gone to a Newington dentist, Thomas Mills, and asked for a guinea for twelve teeth, to which fragments of flesh and jaw were still attached, and which had obviously been removed by force, one of them being badly chipped. Mills testified at the inquest that the teeth had belonged to a boy aged about fourteen or fifteen years.

The chief difficulty of the authorities lay in identifying the body. Several parents of missing children had been brought by the police to look at the corpse, but none had recognized it. A stockbroker testified that it was the body of an Italian boy who wandered the streets with white mice in a cage hanging round his neck, but he then withdrew his evidence, saying that he had since seen the boy he was referring to. After hearing the various alibis of the four prisoners, the inquest jury returned a verdict of wilful murder by person or persons unknown, and added that the strongest suspicion attached to Bishop and Williams.

Searches by police had meanwhile uncovered assorted tools at Bishop's house in Nova Scotia Gardens, including a bradawl with fresh blood on it, as well as a rope with a noose.[9] May's house near the Elephant and Castle produced a bloodstained vest and trousers, but there was doubt as to whether these were connected with the murder.

The boy's body was buried, meanwhile, only – with a grim irony – to be exhumed some days later, when an Italian, Augustine Bruen, was brought to see it, and identified it as that of Carlo Ferreer or Ferrari, whom Bruen had himself brought over to England two years earlier. Bruen was a sort of prototype Fagin, providing slum lodgings for likely lads and sending them out begging in the streets.

Further police searches at the Bishop home revealed torn and bloodstained clothes buried in the garden and pieces of human flesh in the privy, including a woman's scalp. The privy of the empty house next door also produced some bloodstained women's clothing, identified as belonging to a missing middle-aged woman named Frances Pigburn. Head, alias Williams, had lived in this house until a couple of months before, when he had moved in with the Bishops on marrying Bishop's sister. (Bishop had married his step-mother after his father's death, so he had a somewhat complicated relationship with Williams, Bishop's sister also being his step-daughter!)

The Bow Street magistrate duly heard evidence that a scuffle had been heard in Bishop's house on the night of 3 November; that one of Bishop's sons had been seen with a cage containing two white mice; and that Shields, the street porter, had done a previous job for

Bishop and Williams when he had carried a trunk to St Thomas's Hospital, and then to Grainger's, where he had seen the contents – the corpse of a middle-aged woman. May admitted that he had used the bradawl to force out the boy's teeth, but denied knowledge of the murder and said that he had only helped Bishop and Williams to sell the body.

Bishop, Williams and May were committed for trial at the Old Bailey, charged with murdering Carlo Ferrari and another unknown male person. Shields was dismissed. The trial was brief, taking place on 1 December. Four medical experts testified that the boy had been killed by a blow to the back of the neck, and four others stated that they believed the body to be that of the said Carlo Ferrari. The trial concluded with a verdict of guilty against the three men. They were sentenced to death by Chief Justice Tindal, their bodies to be handed over for dissection after execution. Sitting with the Chief Justice on the bench was the sixth son of George IV, Augustus Frederick, Duke of Sussex, of whom more later.

In their cells at Newgate, Bishop and Williams made confessions, Bishop admitting that they had got the idea of murdering their victims from the Burke and Hare case. Both men declared that May was wholly innocent of the murders. May was reprieved, but collapsed from shock on being told, and lived for only a few more months. Bishop's confession was a detailed account of the whole business, and is given in part as Appendix C as an interesting, if repulsive, sidelight on the affair. If wholly true, it shows that Bishop and Williams were found guilty of a murder they did not commit, and by a method they did not use, and were not charged with a murder they *did* commit. Although the police were satisfied that the only body they had in the case was that of Carlo Ferrari, Bishop and Williams were clearly convinced that it was that of a boy who worked as a cattle drover, whom they had seen before at Smithfield.[10]

The end result was the same, however. The two men were brought out to be hanged before a huge and excited crowd on 5 December. Barriers had been erected along Old Bailey to keep the mob back from the scaffold, where the executioner William Calcraft prepared Bishop first and then Williams. When the trap fell, Bishop died instantly, but Williams struggled in his death agonies for some minutes, to the accompaniment of shouting and yelling from the crowd which had gathered from St Sepulchre's church at one end of Old Bailey to Ludgate Hill at the other. Several spectators then rushed the scaffold, breaking down all the barriers and causing many injuries by the pressure of the crowd. A soldier had his arm broken, and some policemen were injured, between twenty and thirty people in all being taken to Bart's Hospital a few yards away. The body of Thomas Williams followed them, after hanging for an hour, for medical attention of a different sort. Bishop's body was awarded to King's College, where Mr Partridge presumably had the satisfaction of taking apart the man who had tried to sell him a murder victim for twelve guineas.

While London was alive with talk about the Bishop and Williams murders, a couple named Edward Cook and Eliza Ross (the latter was also known sometimes as Cook, sometimes as Reardon) were charged with murdering in Whitechapel, in August 1831, an old woman named Caroline Walsh or Welsh, who sold laces and cotton in the streets around Aldgate, and with selling her body to the surgeons. There was insufficient evidence against Cook, though he was well known as a drink-sodden body-snatcher. Nor was there a body in the case, but the chief witness against Eliza Ross, who was Irish, was her twelve-year-old son, who said he had heard his mother tell his father that she had sold the body to the London Hospital. Eliza Ross, 38, was found guilty on this evidence alone and hanged in January 1832. A local publican told a newspaper reporter that she had been well known as a body-snatcher for twelve years. She was also a thief and a violent drunkard. It was said that all the cats in the neighbourhood disappeared because she skinned them for profit. Mr Cook was known to sell the skins of hares to furriers.

Ross had consistently denied murdering Walsh, claiming to the very end that she had left her 'husband' and her son sitting with the old woman and 'never saw her after'. John Bishop, whilst awaiting execution, had been asked what he thought the motive for this murder could be, and replied that it could not have been to sell the corpse, as there was no market for subjects in August. That, however, was not strictly true, and perhaps shows only that Ross was more astute in business than he was.

Eliza Ross's body was delivered to the Royal College of Surgeons, where, as a series of pencil drawings of executed murderers whose bodies were brought to the College for distribution to the anatomy schools. Her head was drawn by William H. Clift, who had also done those of Bishop and Williams.[11] Eliza Ross has been described as 'tall', but Clift, noting that a formal incision was made on the corpse 'from sternum to pubis', before the body was delivered to the London Hospital school for dissection, noted her height as '5 feet'.

A week after the execution of Bishop and Williams, the new Home Secretary, William Lamb, Lord Melbourne, received a petition from the Royal College of Surgeons, whose new President was Robert Keate, pointing out that: 'The large prices which have of late been given for anatomical subjects have operated as a premium for murder,' and warning that if the study of anatomy was to continue, such crimes would increase if something was not soon done. (The full text of the petition is given as Appendix D.) If the tone of this petition was self-righteous, its logic was nevertheless impeccable. It took pains to impress upon the government (yet again, I might add) the contradictions in the law which required the College to examine the student of surgery in his knowledge of human anatomy, while at the same time denying him the legal means of acquiring that knowledge, which was essential to the skilful performance of his duty to the public.

It might be suspected that the President and Council of the College were urged into making this representation by an anonymous letter sent to them, with a copy to the Home Secretary, by one signing himself 'Anatomicus'. This letter, headed London, 29 November 1831, suggested alarmingly (as far as the doctors were concerned) that all dissections should be suspended, in the public interest, until such time as some other arrangements might be made for supplying subjects for teaching anatomy. There was not the shadow of a doubt, the writer claimed, 'but that the practice of Burkeing (horrible to relate!) was adopted at Edinburgh by members of the fraternity of Resurrectionists,' and similar outrages 'transpire here daily.'[12]

Such an alarmist (and inaccurate) view, expressed to a Secretary of State who may not have been as sympathetic to the anatomists as Peel had been, could certainly have stimulated the Royal College's officers into urgent action, if they had not already been well aware that something *was* being done. The petition was in fact more in the nature of a primer to a Home

Secretary perhaps not so well versed in the intricacies of the ghastly situation as his predecessor had been.

A few days later, on 15 December 1831, Henry Warburton presented a revised Bill to the House of Commons. It was a much improved version of the proposal to license anatomists and provide them with a legal supply of subjects. It planned to abolish the practice of dissecting executed murderers, and its provisions obviated the need for new laws to be included against robbing graves. Thus the new Bill successfully dissociated the study of anatomy from crime.

Chapter VII: Terminal Stages

'Of things Bunce feared the most (next to a ghost)
Was law – or any of the legal corps, –
He dropp'd at once his load of flesh and bone,
And, caring for no body save his own,
Bolted, – and lived securely till fourscore,
From never troubling Doctors any more!'

Thomas Hood
The Dead Robbery, c. 1830

Opposition to Warburton's second Bill was led by a persistent new MP, Henry Hunt, representing Preston, who said that one of Dr John Hunter's best pupils, a surgeon named Brown, had told him that Hunter objected to being dissected himself.

Henry Hunt was the radical agitator known as 'Orator Hunt' who had spent several periods in prison, most notably after the Peterloo Massacre, having led the meeting which resulted in the riot. Always a champion of the poor, he became Member of Parliament for Preston in 1830, but lost the seat three years later. He was considered by many to be vain, domineering and capricious. Mr Hunt thought that no young surgeon should enter a school of anatomy, or be allowed to touch a dissecting knife, unless he chose to register his name as an individual willing to give up his body for dissection. This would be the best way of getting rid of that vulgar prejudice of which so much was heard. 'I would recommend,' he said on one occasion, 'in the first place that the bodies of all our kings be dissected, instead of expending seven or eight hundred thousand pounds of the public money for their interment.'

At the Bill's second reading, on 17 January 1832, Mr John Cresset Pelham, the Member for Shropshire, said that he was not so impressed with the indispensable necessity of procuring subjects as some other honourable gentlemen appeared to be. In time of war, he said, the field of battle furnished enough subjects, and there surgeons might obtain a competent knowledge of anatomy.

Joseph Hume, now representing Middlesex, said the Bill would reduce the premium, if not entirely remove the inducement to murder. Mr Hume, who supported the Anatomy Bill as consistently as Henry Hunt opposed it, may be said to have had a vested interest. He had studied medicine as a young man, and was a member of the College of Surgeons of Edinburgh.

Alexander Perceval, the Tory Member for County Sligo, thought the dissection of animals would provide nearly all the advantages which could result from the mere mutilation of human bodies. Less than forty Members were present in the House at this juncture, despite the government's anxiety to rush the Bill through to allay public alarm, and the House adjourned.

The Bill came up again three days later, and the dogged Mr Hunt raised the matter of an artificial corpse invented by a Dr Auzoux in Paris, as a result of which, Hunt claimed, France planned to abolish dissection altogether.[1] His former opposition, Mr Hunt announced, had resulted in attacks on him in the public press, and a threat by a surgeon to dissect him. 'Let him take care, at least,' Mr Hunt said, 'that he does not Burke me first.'

Because of the highly excited state of public feeling

throughout the country, opposition to the proposed measures had considerably diminished, and Hunt's was almost a lone voice in the wilderness by this time. After the second reading and committee stages, Warburton announced that the College of Surgeons in Dublin had requested that the Bill's provisions be extended to Ireland also, and this was agreed. There was also a petition from the Royal College of Surgeons of Edinburgh supporting the Bill. Warburton corrected the damaging impression left by Hunt's erroneous reference to John Hunter. So far from refusing to be dissected, Mr Warburton pointed out, Dr Hunter had expressly directed that his body *should* be dissected, and that certain parts should be prepared and deposited in the College's museum.

Mr Hunt, however, was more impressed by a petition he presented from a surgeon, Robert Thomas Webb, who said that he was an atheist and therefore perfectly indifferent to what became of his body after death; but his wife and family were Christians, and in regard to their feelings he would object to dissection; he therefore prayed for the House not to pass the Anatomy Bill.

Hunt returned to the attack at the third reading, on 11 May. Wax models, he said, had been used for teaching anatomy in Dublin and Paris. Why could it not be done here? It was a disgrace to the medical men of the metropolis that they had not followed the example of their brethren in Dublin and Paris, but required human carcasses to be sold like pigs or sheep.

Mr Sheil, the Member for County Leith, observed that wax models had been used long before in Florence, where they were invented, but that they could never supersede the necessity for actual dissection of human subjects. The Bill received its third reading.

It is surprising, to say the least, that not one of the Bill's opponents had the wit to point out that if the compulsory dissection of some murderers' corpses was indeed a 'further Terror and peculiar Mark of Infamy', this Bill was tantamount to inflicting an identical additional punishment on the poor simply for being poor.

Meanwhile, however, the death had occurred in June of Jeremy Bentham, the political philosopher, who left his body to be dissected in a public gesture to help calm the popular feeling against anatomization, and to show that it was not in any way a kind of penalty inflicted on the helpless poor. The body was duly dissected at the Webb Street school and was then embalmed. It is still preserved at University College, where it sits fully clothed in a glass case.

In the House of Lords, the most impressive speech in favour of Warburton's Bill came from the Duke of Sussex. Referring to the required consent of people to being dissected after death, he said: 'I myself have made a provision of that nature. I have directed that, after death, my body shall be opened and examined, for I have some reason to think that there is a peculiarity in my conformation, the knowledge of which may possibly serve the interests of science. I cannot sit down,' the Duke concluded, 'without expressing my full conviction, that if some arrangements be not speedily made, you will drive the study of anatomy altogether from this country, and compel our medical men to resort to foreign countries for that information which they ought to be able to obtain at home.'[2]

Among the Bill's supporters this time was Lord Macauley, who said: 'If the education of a surgeon should become very expensive, if the fees of surgeons should rise, if the supply of surgeons should diminish, the sufferers would be, not the rich, but the poor in our country villages, who would be left again to mountebanks, and barbers, and old women; to charms and quack medicines ... I think this is a Bill which tends to the good of the people, and which tends especially to the good of the poor.'

The Bill was approved. It received the Royal Assent on 1 August 1832, and became law as *An Act for regulating Schools of Anatomy* (2 and 3 William IV). Its preamble reads:

Whereas a Knowledge of the Causes and Nature of sundry Diseases which affect the Body, and of the best Methods of treating and curing such Diseases, and of healing and repairing diverse Wounds and Injuries to which the Human Frame is liable, cannot be acquired without the Aid of Anatomical Examination: And whereas the legal Supply of Human Bodies for such Anatomical Examination is insufficient fully to provide the Means of such Knowledge; And whereas, in order further to supply Human Bodies for such Purposes, divers great and grievous Crimes have been committed, and lately Murder, for the single Object of selling for such Purposes the Bodies of the Persons so murdered; And whereas therefore it is highly expedient to give Protection, under certain Regulations, to the Study and Practice of Anatomy, and to prevent, as far as may be, such great and grievous Crimes and Murder as aforesaid; be it therefore enacted by the King's most Excellent Majesty, by and with the Advice and Consent of the Lords Spiritual and Temporal, and Commons, in this present Parliament assembled, and by the Authority of the same, That it shall be lawful for His Majesty's Principal Secretary of State for the Time being for the Home Department in that part of the United Kingdom called *Great Britain*, and for the Chief Secretary of *Ireland* in that part of the United Kingdom called *Ireland*, immediately on the passing of this Act, or so soon thereafter as may be required, to grant a Licence to practise Anatomy to any Fellow or Member of any College of Physicians or Surgeons, or to any Graduate or Licentiate in Medicine, or to any Person lawfully qualified to practise Medicine in any Part of the United Kingdom, or to any Professor or Teacher of Anatomy, Medicine, or Surgery, or to any Student attending any School of Anatomy, on Application from such Party for such Purpose, countersigned by Two of His Majesty's Justices of the Peace acting for the County, City, Borough, or Place wherein such Party resides, certifying that, to their Knowledge or Belief, such Party so applying is about to carry on the Practice of Anatomy.

This verbose outline clothed a new law which, though a long time coming, seemed on the face of it a piece of legislative common sense.[3] It provided for the appointment of three inspectors to superintend anatomy schools and make quarterly returns to the Home Office of all bodies dissected. Executors and other persons legally in charge of dead bodies could give them to licensed surgeons and anatomy teachers unless the deceased had expressed conscientious objection to being dissected, but no body could be dissected until forty-eight hours after its death, and then only if a death certificate issued by a surgeon or physician accompanied it. Licensed anatomists were to notify inspectors of the identities of bodies, and the time when received, as well as to confirm that decent interment had taken place after dissection, and not more than six weeks after receipt. The maximum penalty for any offence against these laws was set at three months' imprisonment or a fine of fifty pounds.[4]

The Anatomy Act repealed the law ordering the bodies of executed criminals to be dissected or hung in chains, and substituted hanging in chains or burial within prison precincts. Its passing coincided, however, with the last recorded use of a gibbet, when the corpse of a Leicester bookbinder named Cook, hanged for murder on 11 August, was suspended in iron hoops thirty-three feet above the ground with its head shaved and tarred, but was ordered by the Home Secretary to be removed after only three days.

That same summer also saw the foundation of the first of the authorized London cemeteries (at Kensal Green) which began to replace the overcrowded and evil-smelling churchyards where the resurrection men had been presented with such easy pickings.[5] It was, too, the year in which Charles Hastings, a Worcester doctor, founded the British Medical Association, with its object of 'raising the tone of provincial medical practice'. In fact, 1832 should be celebrated as a year in which Britain took a few tiny steps in its progress toward civilization, in bringing an end to aspects of its national life that were both callous and barbarous, and reducing the 'thousand natural shocks that flesh is heir to'.

Shortly after the passing of the Act, the London lecturers in anatomy, who collectively asserted that they had 'always felt the strongest objection to the practice of Exhumation' and had hitherto 'submitted to it solely from necessity', held a meeting at the Freemasons' Tavern and resolved to support the new law by refusing to employ 'any of those persons who were engaged in the illegal traffic now abolished'. They also appointed a committee to transmit to the schools of anatomy those unclaimed bodies which they hoped would now be obtained with government co-operation, for, they pointed out, 'considerable difficulty and Embarrassment will be felt for some time in procuring a supply of bodies for the furtherance of the business of Medical Education'. The signatories to this resolution comprised Frederick Tyrrell, Edward Stanley, George Dermott, Herbert Mayo and thirteen others.[6]

Although Manchester, Birmingham, Sheffield and Exeter (as well as Oxford and Cambridge) had established medical schools by the 1820s, and Leeds in 1831, it was not until after the passing of the Anatomy Act that schools were founded in other English provincial towns: Hull, Bristol, Nottingham, Newcastle, Liverpool and York all acquired their own schools in the years 1832–4.[7]

The school at Hull was founded in 1832, possibly by James Alderson, who gave the first lectures there, but this school closed down in 1869. Bristol's school was founded in 1833 by Henry Clark, and Nottingham's also came into being in that year, but seems to have been very short-lived. Newcastle's school was founded in 1834, but in 1857 was absorbed into the Medical Faculty of Durham University, the first provincial school outside Oxford and Cambridge to grant degrees in medicine. Liverpool acquired its Royal Institution School in 1834, founded by Doctors Formby and Gill, and this changed its name to the Royal Infirmary School of Medicine ten years later. The medical school at York was founded in 1834 by James Atkinson, surgeon to the York County Hospital and son of Charles Atkinson, who also practised as a surgeon at York. James was somewhat eccentric, and preserved bits and pieces of his patients in a room at the Yorkshire Museum. After his death, the museum promptly got rid of the collection, and the medical school closed down in 1859 as it could not compete with the larger school in Leeds.

All the former horrors by no means disappeared instantly with the passing of the Anatomy Act, as is sometimes implied. Nor was there any optimism in some quarters that the Act would be effective in ending them. Morpeth in Northumberland built its churchyard watch hut as late as 1832; and at Cornhill-on-Tweed the bodies of two men were guarded after their burial in

1844, twelve years after the Act came into force. It was no doubt feared that the new medical school at Newcastle would provide incentive for continued body-snatching.

Hardly a month had passed under the new law before there were riots in Manchester, after the discovery that the well-known surgeon Joseph Jordan, prior to the burial of a young boy who had died in hospital, had cut off the head. The windows of the school in Bridge Street, which Jordan had founded in 1814, were smashed, and a great deal of other damage was done before troops were called out to disperse the rioters.

In Sheffield, in January 1833, the anatomy school was badly damaged by a crowd of people when someone heard a cry of 'murder' from a window. It turned out that it was the caretaker's wife, quarrelling with her drunken husband. In December of that year, the anatomy school at Cambridge was also attacked by a mob.

Six years after the Act, three men were charged with breaking open a vault in Hendon's parish church and severing the head from one of the bodies in it. The case came before the Middlesex Sessions in November 1838. One of the three men was a surgeon, and the mutilated corpse was that of his mother. The case for the defence was that he wanted to investigate the nature and cause of an hereditary disease in order to protect himself and his family from it in the future. The jury found this story hard to swallow, and the three were judged guilty.

Another curious case had occurred at Norwich in that year. On 8 July, a blacksmith, James Maxey, died. He had been employed by a veterinary surgeon, George Perowne, and on the day after his death Mr Perowne called on Maxey's widow and told her that he would pay for her late husband's proper burial as 'a Christian and a gentleman'. He had a coffin sent to the house. On 11 July, Perowne entered the house in Mrs Maxey's absence and took away the coffin (with the body inside it) in his gig. Mrs Maxey went to Mr Perowne and demanded the return of her husband's body, but she was assured that it was all right and that the funeral would take place from his premises on the following day.

When Mrs Maxey turned up at the appointed time with the bearers, the coffin lid was nailed down and she – already suspicious – had the support of her friends the bearers when she insisted on seeing the body. Perowne then flew into a rage, fetched a gun, and threatened to shoot them all if they did not get off his premises. They alleged that, while out in the street, they heard Perowne unfixing the coffin lid and removing large stones! They were eventually let in again and were shown the coffin with the body in it, which they said had been 'cut and hacked' and looked as if it had been anatomized.

Mrs Maxey told this story to the magistrates with Perowne in court drunk, and he was kept in a cell for the night, but next morning he claimed that he had done a deal with Maxey sixteen years earlier for the possession of his body after his death, and that dissection of it had shown that Maxey had died of ossification of the heart. The magistrate pointed out that the law did not recognize ownership in a dead body and that, in any case, Perowne's premises were not licensed for anatomical studies, his profession not requiring him to have knowledge of human anatomy. He was committed for trial at Norwich Assizes on 6 August. In the meantime, however, influential people must have been at work on Perowne's behalf, for when the day of the trial came, he was formally discharged.[8]

A raid on the churchyard at Salcombe Regis in Devon by two surgeons, Mr Hodge and Mr Jeffery, was designed to obtain the body of a labourer's son, a boy named Harding who had died of an interesting brain disease. Whilst they were at work, however, shots rang out from the cottage near the churchyard where the boy's family lived. Both doctors were hit with lead shot, and they dropped their tools and fled. Jeffery said afterwards that they had run all the way back to Sidmouth (a distance of a mile and a half), Jeffery with blood running down his body and leg. On reaching Mr Hodge's house in High Street, the latter spent most of the night extracting shot from his colleague, who had been hit extensively on his right side over the region of the liver. The author of this record could not remember the date of the event, which had been related to him by Mr Jeffery, but thought it was between 1840 and 1850.[9] It may well have been rather earlier than this, in fact. Thomas Hodge, a surgeon of some repute in the Sidmouth area, died in October 1842. The author was also mistaken in supposing that body-snatchers used tools to heave entire coffins out of the ground. These doctors were using the tool previously described at Salcombe Regis, and dropped it when they ran away.

In December 1833, a mob attacked the medical school at Cambridge in the mistaken belief that unlawful means of obtaining bodies were still being employed.[10] Sir George Paget of Cambridge University was fond of telling the story of an Essex farmer who shot a burglar and, having no idea what he ought to do with the body, sent it to Sir George in a box with a note saying simply that he was sending him a man he had shot.

There was a serious disturbance at Sheffield as late as June 1862. It appears that a man with a grudge against the cemetery sexton at Hillsborough spread rumours that bodies were being dug up immediately after interment and sold for dissection. Several coffin plates and a mutilated body found in the cemetery were cited as evidence in support of the allegations, but the authorities explained that old coffin plates were often thrown up in the course of digging new graves, and the corpse was that of a person legitimately dissected in the medical school and sent to the cemetery for burial.

Fuel was added to the flames of local suspicion, however, by the discovery of about twenty coffins in a mass grave, some with bodies in them, and some without. A mob gathered in the evening and started throwing stones at the sexton's house, and then entered it and did much damage before learning that he no longer lived there. The noisy mob made its way to his new home about a mile away and found only his wife at home. They made her leave, saying they intended *her* no harm, and then set about smashing up the furniture and setting fire to it. As the blaze got going, the mob prevented anyone from reaching it to try to save the premises. By the time police and the fire brigade arrived, it was too late, and the house was burnt to the ground, someone in the crowd shouting: 'Let the bugger's den burn; he's built it by selling the dead!' There seems to have been no foundation for these allegations, the coffins and remains found having been either those of stillborn infants buried in a common grave, or those of adults moved there from another part of the cemetery to make way for new graves.[11]

Scotland's die-hard tradition lingered on. Medical students at Aberdeen are said to have stolen a corpse from the kirkyard at Peterculter half a century after the Act, more in a spirit of daring than of science.

Nevertheless, despite all these late flourishes of illicit corpse-dealing, the Anatomy Act put a decisive end to the trade in dead bodies for medical purposes, and without the huge public outcry that many had feared. In June 1833, a Mr William Williams wrote floridly to Sir Astley Cooper: 'Sir, Being full sensible of the uncertainty of this life and the mortality of my animated frame the tabernacle of my soul and of the living spirit that pervades it and under the impression of sentiment that my mind can have already received on the subject of public benefit derived from anatomy, I beg Sir to communicate to you in writing what in substance has already been submitted by personal communication to your Notice and approbation in regard to the body graciously bestowed me by my Maker when my hereafter desertion of that body by its animated tenants of spirit and soul takes place ... '[12]

Not everyone converted to the idea of leaving his or her corpse to medical science felt a compulsion to express the explanation for their decisions in such verbose piousness, but we may see the letter as symbolic of a turn of the tide against dissection, like the dramatic change of attitude that was to occur when cremation was legalized half a century later.

The ultimate failure of the Anatomy Act, however, was that it did *not* solve the problems of the lecturers in obtaining sufficient bodies for their purposes. On the contrary, it actually reduced the number they had available. Dr Arthur Robinson, Professor of Anatomy at Edinburgh University, was able to write in 1921: 'It is well known that the number of unclaimed bodies buried in the United Kingdom every year at the public expense is sufficient to supply all the medical schools with the material necessary for the training of surgeons and physicians, yet there are few if any schools which receive an adequate supply ... ' Dr Robinson put the blame for this situation on local authorities, who customarily evaded the spirit of the Act.[13] In this country, the handing over of bodies was *permissive* on local authorities, whereas in other countries it was *compulsory*.

The improvement in social and financial conditions of

the poor, and the lowering of the death rate by medical advances, ironically worked against the anatomy schools by leading to fewer bodies remaining unclaimed.[14] From about six hundred corpses supplied from various sources in the year after the Act became law, the number had fallen by more than a third within a decade, and so, far from each student dissecting two or three corpses, he was soon lucky to share one corpse with three of his fellows.

Nevertheless, the resurrection men mostly vanished into the obscurity from which they had emerged a century earlier. Though one or two of them earned their livings from more respectable occupations for a time, such as Bill Hollis, who became a hackney coachman, and Naples the diarist, who was given a job in the dissecting room at St Thomas's Hospital, they were usually unable to resist either the drink or the easier money to be made from criminal activities. Naples died of drink. Bill Harnett, who had once been a pugilist like Crouch, died of tuberculosis in St Thomas's. Butler was sentenced to death in Edinburgh in connection with a theft from a mail-coach, but was reprieved. A man named Page, who had sold subjects to Cooper, was hanged for stealing a horse after being informed on, apparently by Hollis, who died in poverty like most of his ilk. Murphy and Jack Harnett were more astute, and accumulated respectable savings from their exploits. Hodgson, the youthful Yorkshire body-snatcher, went to London and tried to earn a living as a 'legal adviser' in Portugal Street, close to the new headquarters of the Royal College of Surgeons, where he was sometimes able, also, to prescribe remedies for his clients' ailments. He died in 1868.

We do not know how the professional resurrection men who had been made redundant felt about those like Burke and Hare, Bishop and Williams, who had muscled in on the scene and brought down the curtain by going too far. It is probable – indeed almost certain – that if no murders had been committed (or at any rate discovered), body-snatching would have continued as a lucrative business for several more years at least, since the government was not anxious to risk alienating its supporters for the sake of a few stolen corpses which were not legally anyone's property.

Although the Anatomy Act ended the careers of body-snatchers as appendages of medical science, the robbing of graves did not entirely disappear, and has hardly yet done so. The idea that dead bodies are not without value in the right quarters persists and will be suppressed only when cremation is made compulsory.

In 1876 an American gang tried to steal the remains of Abraham Lincoln, and intended to return them in exchange for the release of a convicted forger, Ben Boyd. The culprits were caught in the act, and Lincoln's coffin was embedded in steel and concrete some years later. In 1878, Benjamin Harrison, the son of a former US Senator, John Scott Harrison, who had recently died and been buried at North Road, Ohio, had occasion to visit the Ohio Medical College at Cincinnati, and there discovered the body of his father.

In Tasmania in 1869, a native Aborigine, William Lanne, died, and as he was believed to be one of the last of his race, his corpse became the subject of a battle between local scientists and agents of the Royal College of Surgeons in London. A Dr Crowther, representing the latter, severed the head, skinned it, and tried to delay discovery of the theft by substituting another skull in the skin. Enraged local officials then cut off the hands and feet in order to ensure that the Royal College would never get the whole skeleton. The body was then buried, but exhumed later by agents of the local Royal Society. The head, meanwhile, was thrown overboard from the ship carrying it to London, when the stench became intolerable, Dr Crowther having wrapped it in a sealskin.[15]

In Scotland in December 1881, the body of Alexander William Lindsay, twenty-fifth Earl of Crawford and Balcarres, was stolen from the family vault at Dunecht. The thieves demanded a ransom of six thousand pounds. The body was missing for six months, during which bloodhounds and mediums joined police in a search for the remains and the criminals. The corpse was eventually found wrapped in a blanket beneath shallow soil on the family estate. Only one man – a rat-catcher named Soutar – was brought to justice, and was sentenced to five years' penal servitude. His accomplices were never caught.

In November 1888 the remains of the Spanish artist Francisco Goya were exhumed from the cemetery in Bordeaux, where he had been buried in 1828, in order to be returned to his native country and reburied in Madrid. But when the coffin was opened, the skeleton was found to be headless. The skull of Goya has never been seen since, and the reason for its theft remains a mystery.

In March 1978 the body of Charles Chaplin, the great comedian and film director, who had died on Christmas Day 1977, was stolen from his grave in the cemetery at Vevey in Switzerland. The kidnappers wanted 600,000 Swiss francs for its return. They were soon apprehended – a couple of incompetent amateurs, Roman Wardas, a Pole, and Gantcho Ganev, a Bulgarian who had struggled for two hours on the sodden ground of a rainy night to effect the disinterment. They had hidden the body in a shallow grave in a cornfield about twelve miles away. They wanted the money to start their own garage business. Wardas got four and a half years' imprisonment and Ganev an eighteen months' suspended sentence.

We cannot leave the story of the resurrection men

without reconsidering the moral questions arising out of their trade. Some writers in the past have fallen into the easy trap of suggesting that the doctors were entirely altruistic and the grave-robbers totally depraved, and concluding, as one American doctor put it, that the Anatomy Act 'permitted cultured, brave and honourable members of the medical profession to escape the slimy tentacles of the resurrectionists'.[16] Few moral questions are that clear-cut in reality.

The case of Robert Knox was a special one. It was his bad luck that he got involved with Burke and Hare, and his bad judgment that led him to continue his dealings with them. If they had approached Dr Monro, as they had originally intended, instead of being sent to Knox, who can say what the outcome might have been? Monro *may* have acted more or less as Knox did, but it is equally possible, and perhaps more likely, that he would have acted as the excellent Mr Partridge did in London later, and then we would hardly have heard of Burke and Hare at all.

But what about all the other anatomists who were not (as far as we know) involved in any way with the bodies of murder victims? Before 1828, they were not breaking any law of the land in purchasing corpses which had been dug up from churchyards. They were, however, offending the sensibilities of the general public, and in this they were surely guilty of much unprincipled arrogance and presumption. The government having failed to intercede in a situation which was rapidly getting out of hand, the doctors persuaded themselves that they were entitled to violate the beliefs and emotions of the people, especially the poor and bereaved, and in the end to look the other way when it was already clear that lives were being sacrificed. It is evident that the teachers of anatomy were concerned as much for their own careers and incomes as for the furtherance of medical knowledge.

We may also reasonably accuse them of hypocrisy. They purported to be horrified by an enforced association with men whom they freely represented as the lowest dregs of society, but they had voluntarily entered into a trade with them as interdependent partners. The doctors had *themselves* been resurrection men before the professionals appeared on the scene, and were glad enough to employ these men to do their dirty work for them, but now they had the temerity to call them the scum of the earth, because they dug up dead bodies for *money*, whereas the doctors had only done it for *science*!

It may reasonably be asked, 'What could the doctors have done differently?' It is perfectly true that the medical profession had been making representations for many years about their problems in teaching anatomy and training the surgeons the government wanted. But their protests were isolated and lily-livered. What was needed was a concerted effort to present the government of the day with an ultimatum – no corpses, no surgery. The failure of the doctors thus to force the government's apathetic hand resulted from their easy-going preference for the status quo, in which they obtained subjects with few questions asked, and few but the ever-suffering poor were directly affected.

Science is not above the law, whatever visions it may have of long-term benefits to humanity. And if the scientist is engaged in something which the law of the land has not come to terms with, he surely has a clear moral duty to consider the consequences of his actions for the living. The doctors failed to do this, because impatience for knowledge leads science into the error of believing it has no responsibility except to Truth, which as Schopenhauer said, 'can wait, for it has a long life before it'. The unpalatable fact is that the marvellous skills of our highly qualified surgeons today have been gained partly at the expense of widespread fear and distress among ordinary people, especially the poor, who felt themselves to be not the beneficiaries of medical science, but its helpless victims.

In the final analysis, however, the fault for the whole shabby business lies squarely on the shoulders of successive governments. Frederick Lonsdale blamed 'Tory fogyism' for thwarting the progress of medical science. That view is hard to deny, despite the fact that the most dogged opponent of legalized dissection in Parliament was the radical 'Orator Hunt'. It seems unarguable that if class distinction had not been such a powerful element in the way people regarded the evil, much of the public outcry could have been avoided, and medical progress hastened rather than impeded.

At the meeting of the Liverpool Literary and Philosophical Society at which it was resolved to petition Parliament, William Rathbone said that a petition from such a body as theirs would be secure from 'the dangers to which an individual would be exposed who should venture to brave the prejudices of the more ignorant classes of society'; and that airing the question would diminish popular prejudice 'and that morbid sentiment of reverence for the dead which in the present state of public feeling induces even the poor to an excessive expenditure on funerals ... '[17]

This is a revealing statement. The view expressed was far from uncommon among the ruling classes. But if the common man's reverence for the dead was due to ignorance, the answer clearly lay in education. Why is it, then, that no effort was made by any government to persuade people of the error of their old-fashioned beliefs, which ought to be abandoned in their own interests as well as those of society as a whole? Partly because these beliefs were – and remain – among the tenets of a religion which it was in the government's interests to encourage and preserve, and which it had itself propounded in the Murder Act by introducing compulsory dissection as an 'additional punishment' after execution, the idea being to deny murderers the possibility of resurrection on Judgment Day.

It might have been pointed out to the poor and ignorant that their beliefs were being exploited by commercial undertakers, whose business it was to promote reverence for the dead and the desirability of 'respectable' funerals; and that in any case the dead body would rapidly disintegrate when buried, so that if material resurrection on Judgment Day could be effected from a pile of rotting bones, it was hardly to be prevented by dissection of the corpse.

The Christian faith tends towards maintaining a compliant society, so on the rare occasions when its principles are inconvenient to the government, politicians tend to ignore rather than challenge it. Politicians act according to expediency rather than morality. The abandonment of religious obedience would have been a far worse consequence for society's rulers than the loss of support for the government if it had legalized dissection much earlier. But rather than opt for the lesser of the two evils, it chose to do nothing at all, hoping no doubt that the activities of the body-snatchers and the anatomists would never provoke more than occasional local disturbances which the magistrates could deal with, without the need for government interference.

The explanations sometimes offered for government failure to act, such as that it was preoccupied with the more important Reform Bill, are unacceptable. The politicians did not have the foresight to realize the importance of the issue, as is clear from some of the ridiculous speeches made during the passage of the Anatomy Bill through Parliament. It was a sordid and unseemly subject affecting the poor and ignorant rather than the rich, and they preferred to pass by on the other side. Even after the Burke and Hare and the Bishop and Williams murders, the politicians did not think the matter serious enough to merit their close attention. When the government was at last intent on getting the Bill through Parliament, few turned up for the debates.

A change in the law many years earlier to allow unclaimed bodies to be used for teaching anatomy, as well as any donated for the purpose, might not have been widely popular, but it would have been accepted by the British public, if only as a necessary evil, as it had been in so many other countries, much more readily than the unauthorized and offensive raiding of churchyards to maul and dismember the remains of those whom people had been taught – rightly or wrongly – to lay to rest with dignity and the respect due to them.

Instead, even if we go back no further than the beginning of the nineteenth century, the governments of Pitt, Addington, Grenville, Portland, Perceval, Liverpool, Canning, Goderich and Wellington, all of them Tory except one, failed to act in spite of calls for legislation from the medical men, who had become increasingly vociferous towards the end of the Napoleonic wars. Such a law would have prevented not only a great deal of mental agony among the country's poor, but also the deaths of many who died violently and needlessly, and who have no memorials, such as Abigail Simpson, Mary Paterson, Ann McDougal, Mary and Peggy Haldane, Jamie Wilson, Margery Docherty, Caroline Walsh, Fanny Pigburn, and several other victims we know of as well as, undoubtedly, many of whom we know nothing. The fact is that these people were murdered because of inefficient government.

The raising of dead bodies for anatomical purposes was a variation on a very old and lasting theme. The British resurrection men, however, made a considerable mark on nineteenth-century literature, as some of the quotations at the heads of my chapters show. The most famous literary result of the period was Mary Shelley's *Frankenstein*. It was written in Switzerland and published in 1818, when the author was but twenty. She had spent much of her impressionable girlhood in Scotland, and knew of the surgeons' experiments with galvanism as well as the body-snatching business. Dr Frankenstein collects his ghastly raw materials from dissecting rooms, charnel houses and graveyards.

Thomas Love Peacock, in *Crotchet Castle* (1831), represents the Reverend Dr Folliott beating off a pair of ruffians who attacked him, and explaining afterwards that if it had not been for his early gymnastics and his holy rage, 'I should be, at this moment, lying on the table of some flinty-hearted anatomist, who would have sliced and disjointed me as unscrupulously as I do these remnants of the capon and chine ... '

The poets Robert Southey and Thomas Hood reflected the popular feelings of their time. Hood's life spanned the most active period of body-snatching, and he wrote three grimly humorous poems on the subject, one of them entitled 'The Dead Robbery' in which, like Southey, he makes doctors their own victims. Another had the punning title 'Jack Hall', the 'hero' being a body-snatcher who did deals with the doctors over his own body. ('Ten guineas did not quite suffice, And so I sold my body twice.')

David Moir in *Mansie Wauch* and Lord Lytton in *Lucretia* were among other contemporary authors who introduced body-snatchers into their work. Dickens's 'Jeremiah Cruncher' appeared in *A Tale of Two Cities* in 1859, Dickens having been present at the trial of Bishop and Williams. Robert Louis Stevenson's story *The Body-Snatcher*, set partly in the old kirkyard at Glencorse, came out in 1884.

It was, naturally enough, Burke and Hare, rather than the resurrection men, who made the longest-lasting impact, and excited the imaginations of De Quincey, James Bridie and Dylan Thomas, among others. Bridie, himself a doctor (Osborne Henry Mavor, a graduate of Glasgow University), assumed Knox's guilt from the beginning in his play *The Anatomist*, first produced in Edinburgh in 1930.

Mary Shelley had given a disturbing account of Man playing God, exploring the limits of knowledge without regard to the consequences, and Dylan Thomas, more than a century after the events, returned to the theme in *The Doctor and the Devils* and tried to deal with the issue of whether the anatomists' ends justified the means, even to the extent of turning a blind eye to murder. But he embodied a struggle of conscience in Knox which does not seem to have existed in reality.[18]

Perhaps we might allow Thomas Hood the last word on the subject. His contemporary satirical poem 'Mary's Ghost' reflects well enough the real offence, to ordinary and on the whole laudable human feelings, of the business the doctors and the resurrection men were involved in:

> 'Twas in the middle of the night,
> To sleep young William tried;
> When Mary's ghost came stealing in,
>   And stood at his bed-side.
>
> O William dear! O William dear!
>   My rest eternal ceases;
> Alas! my everlasting peace
>   Is broken into pieces.

I thought the last of all my cares
    Would end with my last minute;
But tho' I went to my long home,
    I didn't stay long in it.

The body-snatchers they have come,
    And made a snatch at me;
It's very hard them kind of men
    Won't let a body be!

You thought that I was buried deep,
    Quite decent like and chary,
But from her grave in Mary-bone,
    They've come and boned your Mary.

The arm that used to take your arm
    Is took to Dr. Vyse;
And both my legs are gone to walk
    The hospital at Guy's.

I vowed that you should have my hand,
    But fate gives us denial;
You'll find it there, at Dr. Bell's,
    In spirits and a phial.

As for my feet, the little feet
    You used to call so pretty,
There's one, I know, in Bedford Row,
    The t'other's in the City.

I can't tell you where my head is gone,
    But Doctor Carpue can;
As for my trunk, it's all packed up
    To go by Pickford's van.

I wish you'd go to Mr. P.
    And save me such a ride;
I don't half like the outside place
    They've took for my inside.

The cock it crows – I must be gone!
    My William, we must part!
But I'll be yours in death, altho'
    Sir Astley has my heart.

Don't go to weep upon my grave,
   And think that there I be;
They haven't left an atom there
   Of my anatomie.

Appendix A

The Humble Petition of the Liverpool Literary and Philosophical Society to the Honourable the Commons of Great Britain and Ireland, in Parliament Assembled, dated May 1825

SHOWETH

That without an intimate knowledge of the anatomy of the human body, as it appears to your petitioners, the professors of medicine and surgery are unable to afford any reasonable prospect of stopping the progress of disease, or of remedying the accidents to which the human frame is liable.

That such an intimate knowledge of anatomy is only to be acquired by patient, and laborious, and repeated dissections; and the students of anatomy in this country have, generally, been supplied with bodies by the disinterment of the dead.

That, during the last century, it was declared by the Judges to be an offence at the common law to disinter the dead, even for the purpose of dissection, as being contrary to public decency.

That your petitioners unreservedly admit, that the present system of disinterring the dead is mischievous and disgusting, and that some other plan should, without delay, be adopted in its stead. It is mischievous, because the employment of men in the night time in the secret breach of the laws is a nursery for crime, as the continued commission of one offence leads men, by degrees, to the disregard of all moral obligation; and it is disgusting, because the invasion of the grave offends against the natural feelings of mankind; but your petitioners humbly submit to your honourable House, that until some means shall be devised for supplying anatomical students with subjects, without recourse being had to exhumation, the practice must, necessarily, prevail.

That of late prosecutions for this offence have been very numerous, and most severe sentences have followed conviction; and, in consequence, the number of dead bodies for dissection have considerably diminished, and the operations of the anatomist have been thereby greatly fettered. They have increased, too, the rapacity of the disinterrers of the dead, and have compelled students to leave London and Edinburgh for Dublin and Paris, where the difficulties of acquiring anatomical knowledge are not so great.

That your petitioners beg to suggest, that if the bodies of persons dying in hospitals, workhouses, penitentiaries, and prisons, not claimed by relations or friends willing to incur the expense of their burial, should, by legislative enactment, be delivered over to anatomists before interment, there would be a sufficient number of bodies for anatomical purposes, and the spoliation of the tomb (which, though so brutalizing, is at present necessary) would cease; and provision might be made, in any enactment, for the decent interment of the remains, after the purposes of the anatomist shall have been satisfied.

That your petitioners are aware, that in the minds of the charitable and the humane fears may be entertained, that the dread of dissection might prevent many poor objects from entering into workhouses or public hospitals, whom indigence or malady might naturally lead to seek such an asylum, but your petitioners are strongly of opinion, that if any such feeling should arise, it would be of short continuance only; for the hospitals at Paris, where a similar practice prevails, are always filled. And your petitioners humbly suggest, that bodies are now generally removed from the graves of poor persons, because of the greater facility of getting them; and that the opening of the dead before interment is less revolting to the mind, than their disinterment for the same purpose.

Your petitioners, therefore, humbly pray, that your honourable House will be pleased to take into consideration the difficulties of acquiring anatomical knowledge in this country under the existing laws; and that your honourable House will be pleased to institute such legislative measures, as may supply the students of anatomy in this country with dead bodies, and may, at the same time, put an end to the revolting practice of disinterring the dead.

Appendix B

The Report of the Committee of Investigation into Dr. Knox's dealings with Burke and Hare, dated 13 March 1829

The Committee who, at the request of Dr. Knox, undertook to investigate the truth or falsehood of the rumours in circulation regarding him, have gone into an extensive examination of evidence, in the course of which they have courted information from every quarter. They have been readily furnished with all which they required from Dr. Knox himself, and though they have failed in some attempts to procure evidence, they have in most quarters succeeded in obtaining it, and especially from those persons who have been represented to them as having spoken the most confidently in support of these rumours, and they have unanimously agreed on the following report.

1. The Committee have seen no evidence that Dr. Knox or his assistants knew that murder was committed in procuring any of the subjects brought to his rooms, and the Committee firmly believe that they did not.

2. On the question whether any suspicion of murder at any time existed in Dr. Knox's mind, the Committee would observe that there were certainly several circumstances (already known to the public), regarding

some of the subjects brought by Burke and Hare, which, now that the truth has come out, appear calculated to excite suspicion, particularly the very early period after death at which they were brought to the rooms, and the absence of external marks of disease, together with the opinion previously expressed by Dr. Knox, in common with most other anatomists, of the general abandoned character of persons engaged in this traffic. But, on the other hand, the Committee, after much anxious inquiry, have found no evidence of their actually having excited it in the mind of Dr. Knox, or of any other of the individuals who saw the bodies of these unfortunate persons prior to the apprehension of Burke.

The bodies do not appear in any instance to have borne any external marks by which it could have been known whether they had died by violence or suddenly from natural causes, or from disease of short duration, and the mode of protracted anatomical dissection practised in this and other similar establishments is such as would have made it very difficult to ascertain the causes of death, even if special inquiry had been instituted with that intention.

No evidence whatever has come before the Committee that any suspicion of murder was expressed to Dr. Knox by any one, whether of his assistants or of his very numerous class (amounting to upwards of 400 students), or other persons who were in the practice of frequently visiting his rooms, and there are several circumstances in his conduct, particularly the complete publicity with which his establishment was managed, and his anxiety to lay each subject before the students as soon as possible after its reception, which seem to the Committee strongly to indicate that he had no suspicion of the atrocious means by which they had been procured.

It has also been proved to the satisfaction of the Committee, that no mutilation or disfigurement of any kind was ever practised with a view to conceal the features, or abstract unreasonably any part of the body, the presence of which might have facilitated detection, and it appears clearly that the subjects brought by Burke and Hare were dissected in the same protracted manner as those procured from any other quarter.

3. The Committee have thought it proper to inquire further, whether there was anything faulty or negligent in the regulations under which subjects were received into Dr. Knox's rooms, which gave, or might give, a peculiar facility to the disposal of the bodies obtained by these crimes, and on this point they think it their duty to state their opinion fully.

It appears in evidence, that Dr. Knox had formed and expressed the opinion, long prior to any dealings with Burke and Hare, that a considerable supply of subjects for anatomical purposes might be procured by purchase, and without any crime, from the relations or connections of deceased persons in the lowest ranks of society. In forming this opinion, whether mistaken or not, the Committee cannot consider Dr. Knox to have been culpable. They believe there is nothing contrary to the law of the land in procuring subjects for dissection in that way, and they know that the opinion which Dr Knox had formed on this point, though never acted on to any extent in the profession, has been avowed by others of the highest character in the profession. But they think that Dr. Knox acted on this opinion in a very incautious manner.

This preconceived opinion seems to have led him to give a ready ear to the plausible stories of Burke, who appears from all the evidence before the Committee to have conducted himself with great address and appearance of honesty, as well as in his conversations with Dr. Knox as in his more frequent intercourse with his assistants, and always to have represented himself as engaged in negotiations of that description, and occasionally to have asked and obtained money in advance to enable him and his associate to conclude bargains.

Unfortunately also Dr. Knox had been led, apparently in consequence of the extent and variety of his avocations, to entrust the dealings with persons supplying subjects and the reception of the subjects brought to his assistants (seven in number) and to his doorkeeper indiscriminately. It appears also that he directed or allowed these dealings to be conducted on the understanding (common to him with some other anatomists) that it would only tend to diminish or divert the supply of subjects to make any particular inquiry of the person bringing them as to the place and mode of obtaining them.

In these respects, the Committee considered the practice which was then adopted in Dr. Knox's rooms (whatever be the usage in this or other establishments in regard to subjects obtained in the ordinary way) to have been very improper in the case of persons bringing bodies which had not been interred. They think that the notoriously bad character of persons who generally engage in any such traffic in addition to the novelty and particular nature of the system on which these men professed to be acting, undoubtedly demanded greater vigilance.

The extent, therefore, to which (judging from the evidence which they have been able to procure) the Committee think that Dr. Knox can be blamed on account of transactions with Burke and Hare is, that by this laxity of the regulations under which bodies were received into his rooms, he unintentionally gave a degree of facility to the disposal of the victims of their crimes, which under better regulations would not have existed, and which is doubtless matter of deep and lasting regret, not only to himself but to all who have reflected on the importance and are therefore interested in the prosecution of the study of anatomy. But while they point out this circumstance as the only ground of censure which they can discover in the conduct of Dr. Knox, it is fair to observe, that perhaps the recent disclosures have made it appear reprehensible to many who would not otherwise have adverted to its possible consequences.

John Robinson, *Chairman*   Geo. Ballingall
M.P. Brown   George Sinclair
James Russell   W. Hamilton
J. Shaw Stewart   Thomas Allan
W.P. Allison

Appendix C

The confession made by John Bishop to the Under-Sheriff at Newgate on 4 December 1831, the day before his execution, and confirmed by Williams as altogether true

I, John Bishop, do hereby declare and confess, that the boy supposed to be the Italian boy was a Lincolnshire boy. I and Williams took him to my house about half past ten o'clock on the Thursday night, the 3rd of November, from the Bell, in Smithfield. He walked home with us. Williams promised to give him some work. Williams went with him from the Bell to the Old Bailey watering-house, whilst I went to the Fortune of War. Williams came from the Old Bailey watering-house to the Fortune of War for me, leaving the boy standing at the corner of the court by the watering-house at the Old Bailey. I went directly with Williams to the boy, and we walked then all three to Nova Scotia Gardens, taking a pint of stout at a public-house near Holloway Lane, Shoreditch, on our way, of which we gave the boy a part. We only stayed just to drink it, and walked on to my house, where we arrived about eleven o'clock. My wife and children and Mrs Williams were not gone to bed, so we put him in the privy, and told him to wait there for us. Williams went in and told them to go to bed, and I stayed in the garden. Williams came out directly, and we both walked out of the garden a little way, to give time for the family getting to bed: we returned in about ten minutes or a quarter of an hour, and listened outside the window to ascertain whether the family were gone to bed. All was quiet, and we then went to the boy in the privy, and took him into the house; we lighted a candle, and gave the boy some bread and cheese, and, after he had eaten, we gave him a cup full of rum, with about half a small phial of laudanum in it. (I had bought the rum the same evening at the Three Tuns, in Smithfield, and the laudanum also in small quantities at different shops.) There was no water or other liquid put in the cup with the rum and laudanum. The boy drank the contents of the cup directly in two draughts, and afterwards a little beer. In about ten minutes he fell asleep on the chair on which he sat, and I removed him from the chair to the floor, and laid him on his side. We then went out and left him there. We had a quartern of gin and a pint of beer at the Feathers, near Shoreditch Church, and then went home again, having been away from the boy about twenty minutes. We found him asleep as we had left him. We took him directly, asleep and insensible, into the garden, and tied a cord to his feet to enable us to put him up by, and I then took him in my arms, and let him slide from them headlong into the well in the garden, whilst Williams held the cord to prevent the body going altogether too low in the well. He was nearly wholly in the water in the well, his feet just above the surface. Williams fastened the other end of the cord round the paling, to prevent the body getting beyond our reach. The boy struggled a little with his arms and his legs in the water; the water bubbled for a minute. We waited till these symptoms were past, and then went in, and afterwards I think we went out, and walked down Shoreditch to occupy the time, and in about three-quarters of an hour we returned and took him out of the well, by pulling him by the cord attached to his feet. We undressed him in the paved yard, rolled his clothes up, and buried them where they were found by the witness who produced them. We carried the boy into the wash-house, laid him on the floor, and covered him over with a bag. We left him there, and went and had some coffee in Old Street Road, and then (a little before two on the morning of Friday) went back to my house. We immediately doubled the body up, and put it into a box, which we corded so that nobody might open it to see what was in it; and then went again and had some more coffee in the same place in Old Street Road, where we stayed a little while, and then went home to bed – both in the same house, and to our own beds as usual; we slept till about ten o'clock on Friday morning, when we got up, took breakfast together with the family, and then went both of us to Smithfield, to the Fortune of War – we had something to eat and drink there. In about half-an-hour May came in – I knew May – but had not seen him for about a fortnight before, – he had some rum with me at the bar, Williams remaining in the tap-room ...

[*Two attempts to sell the body during the day failed, then ...*]

about six o'clock, we all three went in the chariot to Nova Scotia Gardens; we went into the wash-house, where I uncorded the trunk, and shewed May the body. He asked, 'how are the teeth?' I said I had not looked at them. Williams went and fetched a brad-awl from the house, and May took it and forced the teeth out; it is the constant practice to take the teeth out first, because, if the body be lost, the teeth are saved; after the teeth were taken out, we put the body in a bag, and took it to the chariot; May and I carried the body, and Williams got first into the coach, and then assisting in pulling the body in ...

[*Further attempts to sell the body ended in success. Bishop made a further declaration saying that May knew nothing of the murder.*]

I have known May as a body-snatcher for four or five years, but I do not believe he ever obtained a body except in the common course of men in the calling – by stealing from the graves. I also confess that I and Williams were concerned in the murder of a female – whom I believe to have been since discovered as Fanny Pigburn – on or about the 9th of October last. I and Williams saw her sitting about eleven or twelve o'clock at night on the step of a door in Shoreditch, near the church. She had a child four or five years old on her lap. I asked her why she was sitting there. She said she had no home to go to, for her landlord had turned her out into the street. I told her that she might go home with us, and sit by the fire all night. She said she would go with us, and she walked with us to my house, in Nova Scotia Gardens, carrying her child with her. When we got there we found the family abed, and we took the woman and lighted a fire, by which we all sat down together. I went out for beer, and we all took beer and rum (I had brought the rum from Smithfield in my pocket); the woman and her child laid down on some dirty linen on the floor, and I and Williams went to bed. About six o'clock next morning I and Williams told her to go away, and to meet us at the London Apprentice in Old-Street Road, at one o'clock. This was before our families were up. She met us again at one o'clock at the London Apprentice, without her child. We gave her some half-pence and beer, and desired her to meet us again at ten o'clock at night at the same place. After this we bought rum and laudanum at different places, and at ten o'clock we met the woman again at the London Apprentice, she had no child with her. We drank three pints of beer between us there, and stayed there about an hour. We would have stayed there longer, but an old man came in whom the woman said she knew, and she did not like him to see her there with any body; we therefore all went out; it rained hard, and we took shelter under a door-way in the Hackney Road for about an hour. We then walked to Nova Scotia Gardens, and Williams and I led her into No. 2, an empty house adjoining my house. We had no light. Williams stepped into the garden with the rum and laudanum, which I had handed to him; he there mixed them together in a half-pint bottle, and came into the house to me and the woman, and gave her the bottle to drink; she drank the whole at two or three draughts; there was a quartern of rum, and about half a phial of laudanum; she sat down on the step between two rooms in the house, and went off to sleep in about ten minutes. She was falling back; I caught her to save her fall, and she laid back on the floor. Then Williams and I went to a public-house, got something to drink, and in about half-an-hour came back to the woman; we took her cloak off, tied a cord to her feet, carried her to a well in the garden and thrust her into it headlong; she struggled very little afterwards, and the water bubbled a little at the top. We fastened the end to the pailings to prevent her going down beyond our reach, and left her and took a walk to Shoreditch and back, in about half-an-hour; we left the woman in the well for this length of time, that the rum and laudanum might run out of the body at the mouth. On our return we took her out of the well, cut her clothes off, put them down the privy of the empty house, carried the body into the wash-house of my own house, where we doubled it up and put it into a hair-box, which we corded and left there.

[Details follow of hiring a street porter to carry the box to St Thomas's, where they were unable to sell the body at once, so took it to Grainger's Anatomical Theatre, where they sold it for eight guineas. About a fortnight later, they murdered a boy about ten named Cunningham in the same manner, and sold the body to St Bartholomew's Hospital for eight guineas.]

Until the transactions before set forth, I never was concerned in obtaining a subject by the destruction of the living. I have followed the course of obtaining a livelihood as a body-snatcher for twelve years, and have obtained and sold, I think, from 500 to 1,000 bodies; but I declare, before God, that they were all obtained after death, and that, with the above exceptions, I am ignorant of any murder for that or any other purpose.

Appendix D

Petition of the Royal College of Surgeons in London to the Viscount Melbourne, His Majesty's Principal Secretary of State for the Home Department, dated 10 December 1831

My Lord,

The undersigned Members of the Council of the Royal College of Surgeons in London, have the honor of addressing Your Lordship on a Subject of painful Interest to the whole Community, but especially to the Members of the medical Profession.

The Royal College of Surgeons are empowered by their Charter to examine certain Individuals as to their knowledge of Surgery, and they are especially required to institute such examination respecting those who are Candidates for the situation of Surgeon in the Army and Navy.

It is not possible that anyone should be properly qualified to practise in this department of the healing Art who has not obtained a due knowledge of Human Anatomy, and explored with his own hand the structure of the dead body; proofs of their having done so have, therefore, been always required of Candidates who have presented themselves for examination.

The Council believed that they could not properly perform their duty to their Sovereign from whom the College received its Charter, nor to the Public for whose benefit it was granted, without insisting on the study of Anatomy by dissection as the most important part of surgical education.

They have however been aware that some serious objections might be urged to the course which they have ventured to take.

In the present state of the common law, as it is construed by the law authorities, the Individual who dissects a human body, or even has it in his possession for any other purpose than that of burial, is guilty of a misdemeanour unless it be the body of a Malefactor hanged for Murder.

Bodies used for dissection in the anatomy schools have necessarily been procured by illegal means, by the invasion of consecrated ground and the disturbance of graves, in a way disgusting to society at large and especially offensive to the friends and relatives of the deceased.

The Regulations of the Council have therefore had a tendency to encourage both Teachers and Students to a direct violation of the Law, and to establish in the Procurers of dead bodies, a set of Men living by practices which are revolting to the feelings of Society, exposed to the hatred and contempt of those around them and likely, by the joint operation of these causes, to become trained and gradually habituated to the commission of still greater crimes.

The Council felt that they could only do what was on the whole for the best in the dilemma in which they were placed:- The circumstances which have just been enumerated did not escape their attention, and have continually excited their most deep regret. But on the other hand they were called upon to regard the obligations of their Charter. They were aware that the want of properly educated Surgeons would prove a serious evil to the public. However much they might be inclined to encourage the use of preserved parts and models as subsidiary means of teaching Anatomy they were convinced that these are of themselves quite inadequate to afford that minute, complete, and accurate knowledge which is necessary in surgical practice, and which the Student acquires by dissection.

The Council further submit that they have laboured under much embarrassment from the inconsistencies and contradictions of the law itself, which at the same time that it declares the Student to be guilty of a misdemeanour if he attempts to obtain anatomical knowledge, renders him also, when afterwards engaged in practice, liable to a civil action on account of any mistake which his ignorance of Anatomy may lead him to commit.

But whatever may have been the extent of the difficulties which have heretofore obstructed the Council in the execution of their duty they may well be regarded as insignificant when compared with those which they have to encounter at the present moment.

The large prices which have of late been given for anatomical subjects have operated as a premium for murder. If the Council of the College continue to require that those who present themselves for examination shall have studied practical Anatomy, who can venture to say that crimes similar to those which have just now filled the public with dismay, will not be again committed? More Criminals will undoubtedly arise; new Victims will be added to the list; and the medical Profession will be, necessarily, degraded from the high station which it ought to hold, as having in its relations to society no object but that of conferring benefit to others.

The Council have no expectation, while the law remains as it is at present, and surgical students continue to cultivate the science of Anatomy, that any means can be contrived which will prevent a repetition of the horrible offences to which they have just alluded. Attention and constant suspicion on the part of the Teachers may effect much but not all that is required.

It is vain to imagine it is always possible to distinguish the body of a person who has been murdered from that of one who has died a natural death.

The very Individuals who have lately suffered on the scaffold would probably have escaped detection if they had been more circumspect and wary in their conduct; Nor can all the precautions with which it is desirable that the study of Anatomy should be conducted be adopted under the existing Laws.

In the other Countries of Europe Anatomy is taught only under a License, and in certain places appointed by the Government, and an exact register is preserved of all the bodies consigned for dissection. But it is a contradiction to suppose that any such license can be granted or such register preserved in this Country, where the study of Anatomy is barely tolerated, and where not only the Procurers of dead bodies but the anatomical Teachers and Students are alike engaged in illegal pursuits.

In offering this Representation to His Majesty's Government, the Council are not without hopes that some plan may be devised by the Legislature calculated to remove the serious evil of which they now complain. At the same time they beg leave to declare on their own part, and on that of all the other Members of their profession who are now in practice, with the exception of the very few who devote themselves to the laborious and often unprofitable task of teaching Anatomy, that the Question is one in which they have no direct or personal interest.

Whether Anatomy be taught legally or illegally, or not

at all, does not concern the existing race of practitioners in medicine or Surgery who have completed the period of their education, but it deeply concerns the Public, and it is under a strong sense of the evils which society may ultimately experience and from a desire conscientiously to perform their duties, that the Council of the College have ventured to make this demand on your Lordship's patience and attention at a moment, which on an occasion of less importance, they should have deemed unseasonable.

Robt. Keate	President	
John P. Vincent	) Vice	Samuel Cooper
Geo. Ja^s. Guthrie	) Presidents	Thos. Copeland
William Blizard		John Howship
Astley Cooper		James Briggs
W^m. Lynn		W^m. Lawrence
I.A. Hawkins		B.C. Brodie
Anthony Carlisle		Benjn. Travers
Hon. Leigh Thomas		Henry Earle
Anthony White		Charles Bell
John Goldwyer Andrews		Joseph Swan

Notes

Notes to Chapter I

1 *The Nazarene Gospel Restored* (Cassell, 1953)
2 In *The Civil Wars*
3 Apuleius: *The Golden Ass* (Penguin edn, 1950)
4 Tacitus: *The Annals of Imperial Rome* (Penguin edn, 1956)
5 *The Duchess of Malfi*
6 I have taken most of these examples of doubtful medicine from Keith Thomas: *Religion and the Decline of Magic*; and R. Holmes: *Witchcraft in British History*
7 Sir George Clark thus quotes A. Broun (1691) in *A History of the Royal College of Physicians*
8 John Aubrey: *Brief Lives* (Penguin edn, 1972)
9 Georgio Vasari: *The Lives of the Artists* (Penguin edn, 1965)
10 In an undated draft letter Leonardo refers to being hindered from practising anatomy in Rome, evidently by the Pope's order. Kenneth Clark says that one Giovanni degli Specchi 'found a means of reporting Leonardo's studies of anatomy to the Pope and having them stopped.' (Kenneth Clark: *Leonardo da Vinci*, Cambridge University Press, 1939)
11 John Stow: *The Survey of London* (Everyman's Library edn, 1956)
12 The cadavers in Rembrandt's famous paintings of lectures given by succeeding Praelectors of Anatomy at Amsterdam's College of Surgeons, Nicolaes Tulp and Johannes Deijman, have been identified as the bodies of Adriaan Adriaansz, a twenty-eight-year-old from Leiden known as *het Kint* ('the child'), who was hanged in January 1632; and (in the picture reproduced in this book) Joris Fonteyn from Diest, nicknamed *Black Jan*, hanged for theft in January 1656.
13 Zola: *Thérèse Raquin*
14 Aubrey, *op cit*
15 Dickens: *The Uncommercial Traveller*
16 *Notes and Queries*, 10 May 1980

Notes to Chapter II

1 G.A.G. Mitchell: *The Medical History of Aberdeen and its Universities* Lecture, printed in Aberdeen University Review, Spring 1958
2 I ought to point out that many of the anecdotes in this and subsequent chapters are beyond verification at this distance of time, but they are given here as popular rumours or fanciful newspaper accounts reflecting the general atmosphere and public feeling of the period. Fear and ignorance are the parents of imagination and exaggeration, and each reteller of a tale tends to want a larger margin of profit on it, resulting in embroidery of the truth for the sake of effect.
3 The story as told by one of the students concerned is repeated in G. Munro Smith: *A History of the Bristol Royal Infirmary*
4 A. Ash and J.E. Day: *Immortal Turpin* (Staples Press, 1948)
5 Quoted in Arthur Koestler: *Reflections on Hanging* (Gollancz, 1956)
6 G. Munro Smith, *op cit*
7 One version of this story was given by A. Macalister in a lecture on *The History of the Study of Anatomy at Cambridge* in 1891, from which it would appear that the dissection was already well advanced when Sterne was recognized. The reburied remains were still not allowed to rest in peace. They were removed again in 1969 to be buried once more, at Coxwold in North Yorkshire where Sterne had been rector, when the London churchyard was dug up for redevelopment.
8 *Scots Magazine*, March 1742
9 Strictly speaking, 'resurrection man' may be defined a little more precisely than 'body-snatcher', the latter sometimes snatching bodies which had not yet been buried, whereas 'resurrection man' clearly implies raising from the grave.
10 *Scots Magazine*, July 1742
11 *Scots Magazine*, February 1752
12 Quoted by Peter Linebaugh in his essay 'The Tyburn Riots Against the Surgeons' in *Albion's Fatal Tree*
13 G. Munro Smith, *op cit*

Notes to Chapter III

1 Article in *Eastern Daily Press*, 21 January 1921
2 Doris Jones-Baker: *Old Hertfordshire Calendar* (Phillimore, 1974)
3 *The Quarterly Review*, vol. 23, 1820
4 J. Cramer: *A History of the Police of Portsmouth* (Portsmouth City Council, 1967)
5 According to Frederick Burgess in *English Churchyard Memorials* (Lutterworth Press, 1963)
6 This diary or log book was presented to the Royal College of Surgeons by Sir Thomas Longmore in 1870, he having bought it from the body-snatcher himself so long before that he could not

remember the man's name! The diary consists of 16 *leaves* (i.e. 32 pages, not 16 pages as other writers have it). They are carefully ruled and, in the earlier part at least, written in a legible and flowing hand. Naples was the son of a stationer and bookseller. The diary was edited for publication by James Blake Bailey, then librarian of the College (and no relation to the present author).

7 Writers who have relied on J.B. Bailey's published version, rather than the original manuscript, have not been aware of the dramatic change in the appearance of the manuscript after the summer of 1812. Up to that point, the pages are very neat. After the summer break, the writing and orderly layout of the pages deteriorated. Was this due to drink, to illness, or simply to sudden lack of interest in such laborious paperwork?

8 It is necessary to treat these Scottish stories with some caution. They were told by Alexander Leighton, in *The Court of Cacus*, at second- or third-hand many years after the supposed events, and may have been enhanced, if not actually invented, by the author's vivid imagination.

9 This version of the story is told by John Latimer: *The Annals of Bristol in the 19th Century*

10 The rumour seems to have been started by an anonymous *Exposure of the Present System of obtaining Bodies for Dissection, etc.*, published in London in 1829

11 *The Kaleidoscope*, 24 October 1826

12 Broadsheet in Bristol Record office

13 *Glasgow Herald*, 10 June 1814; and Peter Mackenzie: *Old Reminiscences of Glasgow*

14 *Liverpool Mercury*, 3 May 1822

15 Quoted in V. Mary Crosse: *A Surgeon in the Early Nineteenth Century*

16 *Bristol Gazette*, 7 November 1822; *Bristol Journal*, 1 February and 19 April 1823

Notes to Chapter IV

1 According to Thomas H. Bickerton in *A Medical History of Liverpool* (1936)

2 Sir Humphrey Rolleston: *Provincial Medical Schools a Hundred Years Ago* (Cambridge University Medical Magazine, 1932)

3 *Bristol Mirror*, 30 October 1819; and G. Munro Smith, *op cit*

4 For the Sunderland stories I am indebted to an article by Sidney Sterck in the *Newcastle Journal*, 1964

5 Articles in *Eastern Daily Press*, 21 January 1921; and *Eastern Evening News*, 17 August 1973

6 *Liverpool Mercury*, 6 and 13 June 1823

7 *Manchester Guardian*, 21 February 1824

8 J. Cramer, *op cit*

9 Herbert W. Tompkins: *Highways and Byways in Hertfordshire* (Macmillan, 1902)

10 Manuscript in Library of the Royal College of Surgeons

11 Minutes of meetings of the Liverpool Literary and Philosophical Society, 4 February, 6 May and 7 October 1825

12 *Lancaster Gazette*, 7 October 1826

13 *Liverpool Mercury*, 13 and 20 October 1826; 3 and 10 November 1826; 26 January 1827

14 *Nottingham Journal*, 27 January 1827

15 The details of this case are taken from an undated nineteenth-century pamphlet, *The Trial of John Eaton*, printed and published in Manchester by J. Pratt, in which it is stated that the Manchester newspapers suppressed the story at the time of its occurrence.

16 *Liverpool Mercury*, 26 October 1827, and 15 February 1828. William Gill was a respected surgeon in Liverpool, and was instrumental in establishing the city's Royal Institution School of Medicine and Surgery in 1834, becoming one of its first lecturers in anatomy, together with Richard Formby.

17 G. Munro Smith, *op cit*

18 The School of Anatomy in Great Windmill Street was founded by the great William Hunter (elder brother of John) and was the first purpose-built anatomy school in London. At the time of the Select Committee, it was under the proprietorship of Charles Bell, soon to be succeeded by Herbert Mayo. Part of the Lyric Theatre is now on the site, and there is a plaque to this effect near the stage door.

Richard Dugard Grainger was proprietor of the school in Webb Street founded in 1819 by his brother Edward, who had died in 1824.

Frederick Tyrrell ran the school in Aldersgate Street which he had founded in 1825. Tyrrell and Edward Grainger had both been pupils of Astley Cooper.

Joseph Constantine Carpue was founder of the school in Dean Street, where he taught until about 1830, and James Bennett was part-proprietor there. Carpue had been a strong advocate of importing bodies from France, where they were cheap and plentiful.

George Darby Dermott had been an assistant to Joshua Brookes, and ran a school in Gerrard Street.

I have not traced who Mr Sleigh was. Did the Committee's clerk record the name wrongly, or did Sir Astley mean F.C. Skey, who was a lecturer at Tyrrell's school in Aldersgate Street? Probably the latter. Sir Astley was not a man to be bothered with precise language. He was inclined, for instance, to say 'prostrate' when he meant 'prostate', and having told the Select Committee that there were ten teachers of anatomy in London, he proceeded to list eleven.

19 I have made some effort to find out who these pseudonymous resurrection men really were, but to no avail. There seem to be no surviving background papers to the work of the Select Committee in the Public Record Office or elsewhere. (I learn from Dr Ruth Richardson's *Death, Dissection and the Destitute* that they were

destroyed in 'a disastrous fire at the Houses of Parliament in 1834'. This was the famous fire of 16 October of that year which destroyed the Old Palace of Westminster and which was painted by Turner.)

Probably the identities of these witnesses were known only to Henry Warburton and one or two others, and no record of their names was made. The assumption that C.D. was Naples seems well founded (but see below). I am convinced, however, that A.B. was not Crouch. In view of his evidence on the greater tenderness of the Irish than the English towards their dead, A.B. was surely an Irishman! It might well have been Murphy, who was a relatively polite and intelligent man, unlike Crouch, who was aggressive and objectionable. The identification with Crouch seems to have been made mainly on the grounds that he had retired by this time and had nothing to lose by appearing before the Select Committee, but all three of the men who gave evidence were granted immunity from prosecution. Naples was certainly still working.

20 Some doubt about the identity of C.D. must arise from the fact that the diary we know of contains no breakdowns or totals of corpses obtained and sold, such as to enable C.D. unhesitatingly, it seems, to answer the questions put to him. The other most likely keeper of an accurate record of his business dealings for those years was undoubtedly Crouch.

Notes to Chapter V

1 *Blackwood's Magazine*, March 1829
2 *Edinburgh Evening Courant*, 7 February 1829
3 This was a trifle hypocritical on Sir Walter's part. He is known to have been an avid reader of murder trials himself, and collected broadsides and other literature relating to them. He was also a member of the audience at Burke's execution.
4 According to Lonsdale, Knox's biographer.
5 This uncorroborated story seems to be solely attributable to J.B. Atlay in *Famous Trials of the Century* (Grant Richards, 1899)

Notes to Chapter VI

1 As well as Knox, the surgeons Thomas Wharton Jones, William Fergusson and Alexander Miller, as well as William Pulteney Alison, Professor of the Theory of Physics at the University of Edinburgh, were listed as witnesses, but not one of them was called to give evidence.
2 *Edinburgh Evening Courant, op cit*
3 Betty MacQuitty: *The Battle for Oblivion* (Harrap, 1969)
4 *A Letter to the Lord Advocate Disclosing the Accomplices, Secrets and Other Facts Relative to the Late Murders; With a Correct Account of the*

Manner In Which The Anatomical Schools Are Supplied With Subjects. Published in Edinburgh in 1829 under the pseudonym 'The Echo of Surgeons' Square'. There is no doubt that the writer was David Paterson.

5 Henry Cockburn: *Memorials of his Time*

6 In *The Life of Sir Robert Christison, Bart.*, edited by his sons in two volumes

7 Sessions Reports, Devon Record Office, and *Exeter Flying Post*, 9 and 16 December 1830

8 The information about Hodgson is taken from various newspaper cuttings in the Central Library, Leeds

9 Nova Scotia Gardens no longer exists. It lay on the north side of a notorious slum area between Shoreditch and Bethnal Green known locally as 'the Nichol', and by the middle of the century had become a stinking rubbish dump. The whole area was demolished and redeveloped during later Victorian slum clearances. The Bunhill Fields burial ground was half way between this area and St Bartholomew's Hospital.

10 If the boy was killed by a blow across the upper part of the spine, as medical witnesses alleged, there was hardly any point in trying to drown him, and he would not have struggled in the water. A curious veracity is given to Bishop's confession by the erroneous belief that hanging a body upside-down would cause the contents of the stomach to run out at the mouth.

11 This little-known rogues' gallery is in the Library of the Royal College of Surgeons.

12 Home Office papers in the Public Record Office, HO 44/24

Notes to Chapter VII

1 The workers at the Paris factory where Dr Auzoux manufactured his models were said at the time to be 'as familiar with anatomy as a painter is with the colours on his palette' – an assertion about which we may reasonably entertain some doubts.

2 In the event, the Duke was not dissected. No doubt the royal family had something to say about that. A post-mortem was conducted, however, which concluded that the Duke had died of erysipelas. But see below, note 5.

3 Dr Ruth Richardson (*op cit*) has taken strong exception to it. But it is very difficult to see what alternative could have been devised that would have been any more acceptable at the time.

4 The Act remained in force for more than a hundred and fifty years with only one minor amendment. The Anatomy Act 1871 (34 Vict.) allowed the Home Secretary to vary the period of time within which certificates of interment were to be provided to inspectors. The Anatomy Act 1984 repealed the Acts of 1832 and 1871, substituting provisions which tighten up the law in certain details, allow for

cremation of remains as well as burial, and provide for the greater length of time that bodies or parts of bodies can now be preserved with the benefits of refrigeration, not available to the nineteenth-century anatomists.

5 Nine years later, in 1843, the Duke of Sussex was buried, by his own wish, in Kensal Green Cemetery, thus helping to quell some public opposition to the new public cemeteries as well as to dissection. He had suffered all his life from painful paroxysms which mystified his physicians, but are now thought to have been symptoms of a hereditary disease of the royal family, porphyria. (See Ida MacAlpine and Richard Hunter: *George III and the Mad-Business*.)

6 Copy in Public Record Office, HO 44/25

7 There are, at the time of writing, thirty-four medical schools in Britain where anatomy is taught. Fourteen of them are in London and five in Scotland. There are also thirteen post-graduate medical centres teaching anatomy. (Information from H.M. Inspector of Anatomy.)

8 Article in *Eastern Daily Press*, 21 January 1921

9 P.O. Hutchinson: *A History of the Town, Parish, and Manor of Sidmouth*. Unpublished MS in Devon Local Studies Library, Exeter

10 Rolleston, *op cit*

11 *Sheffield Telegraph*, June 1862

12 Letter among Sir Astley Cooper's papers in the Library of the Royal College of Surgeons

13 Appendix to the volume on Burke and Hare in the 'Notable British Trials' series

14 Nevertheless, according to Dr Neville Goodman, 97% of the country's supply of subjects in 1941-2 came from institutions, and only 3% from bequests. (*The Supply of Bodies for Dissection* – lecture to the Royal College of Surgeons, published in the *Lancet*, 20 May 1944.)

15 Robert Hughes: *The Fatal Shore* (Collins Harvill, 1987)

16 James Moores Ball, M.D., in *The Sack-'Em-Up-Men*

17 Minutes of Liverpool Literary and Philosophical Society meeting, 4 February 1825

18 Dylan Thomas's film script *The Doctor and the Devils* was written in 1941, but has only recently been filmed with a script by Ronald Harwood based on Thomas's original. This was published in 1953 by Dent.

Select Bibliography

The following are the chief books and official publications I have relied on for the social background of the period, debates in Parliament, and the more widely documented details of body-snatching and the murders arising from the trade in corpses. Newspapers, journals and other sources are given in the notes.

Norman Adams, *Dead and Buried: the horrible history of bodysnatching*, Impulse Books, 1972
James Blake Bailey (Ed), *The Diary of a Resurrectionist*, Swan Sonnenschein, 1896
James Moores Ball, *The Sack-'Em-Up-Men*, Oliver & Boyd, 1928
Sir Norman Birkett (Ed), *The Newgate Calendar*, Folio edn, 1974
Henry Cockburn, *Memorials of his Time*, A. & C. Black, 1856
Horace Bleackley, *The Hangmen of England*, Chapman & Hall, 1929
Sir George Clark, *A History of the Royal College of Physicians*, Oxford University Press, 1966
Hubert Cole, *Things for the Surgeon*, Heinemann, 1964
Robert Christison, *The Life of Sir Robert Christison, Bart.*, W. Blackwood, 1885
Bransby Cooper, *The Life of Sir Astley Cooper, Bart.*, John W. Parker, 1843
V. Mary Crosse, *A Surgeon in the Early Nineteenth Century*, E. & S. Livingstone, 1968
M. Dorothy George, *London Life in the Eighteenth Century*, Kegan Paul, Trench, Trubner, 1925
Arthur Griffiths, *The Chronicles of Newgate*, Bracken Books edn, 1987
Peter Hay et al, *Albion's Fatal Tree*, Allen Lane, 1975
Mrs Basil Holmes, *The London Burial Grounds*, Fisher Unwin, 1896
R. Holmes, *Witchcraft in British History*, Muller, 1974
Alexander Leighton, *The Court of Cacus*, Houlston & Wright, 1861
Henry Lonsdale, *A Sketch of the Life and Writings of Robert Knox, the Anatomist*, London, 1870

John Latimer, *The Annals of Bristol in the 19th Century*, Kingsmead Reprints ed, 1970

Ida MacAlpine & Richard Hunter, *George III and the Mad-Business*, Allen Lane, 1969

George MacGregor, *The History of Burke and Hare, and of the Resurrectionist Times*, Thomas D. Morison, 1884

Peter Mackenzie, *Old Reminiscences of Glasgow*, Forrester, 1890

Roy Porter, *English Society in the Eighteenth Century*, Penguin, 1982

F.N.L. Poynter (Ed), *The Evolution of Medical Education in Britain*, Pitman, 1966

Isobel Rae, *Knox the Anatomist*, Oliver & Boyd, 1964

Ruth Richardson, *Death, Dissection and the Destitute*, Routledge & Kegan Paul, 1987

William Roughead (Ed), *Burke and Hare (Notable British Trials)*, William Hodge, 1921

G. Munro Smith, *A History of the Bristol Royal Infirmary*, Arrowsmith, 1917

Keith Thomas, *Religion and the Decline of Magic*, Weidenfeld & Nicolson, 1971

Cecil Howard Turner, *The Inhumanists*, Alexander Ouseley, 1932

Sidney Young (Ed), *The Annals of the Barber-Surgeons of London*, Blades, East & Blades, 1890

Hansard, Parliamentary Debates, 1829–32

Report from the Select Committee on Anatomy, 1828

An Act for regulating Schools of Anatomy, 2 and 3 Will. IV, c. 75, 1832

Index